Make Your

Faith Work

Other Books by Louis H. Evans

THE KINGDOM IS YOURS

YOUTH SEEKS A MASTER

LIFE'S HIDDEN POWER

THIS IS AMERICA'S HOUR

YOUR MARRIAGE—DUEL OR DUET?

Make Your

Faith Work

A Letter from James

Louis H. Evans

FLEMING H. REVELL COMPANY

To
Robert and Lauralil Evans Deats
in tribute to the inspiration
of their faith

Contents

Foreword

Who was the "James" who wrote The General Epistle of James, in our Bible?

There are many theories about it. Some say it was James, the brother of John and one of the sons of Zebedee. Others say he was James, the son of Alpheus.

But the best evidence favors the theory that the author was James, the brother of the Lord. Most competent scholars now agree on that, and it is good that they do, for this James is perfect for the role. His knees, men said, were calloused as a camel's, from long praying. The scribes and Pharisees hated him, and the people loved him. He became such a leader in the early church that the great Paul came to him, thrice, for advice.

If the brother of Jesus was the author—and we proceed on that well-established premise—then the Epistle he wrote becomes something more than merely interesting, for it contains the conclusions of a brother about a divine Brother. What could be more intimate, more revealing? Brothers are always hypersensitive to what their own think and say about them. "What does

[9]

‚your brother think of you?" is a question that goes into your heart like a knife. So what James says about Jesus, about His faith and works, would go deep.

Now it is apparent that James did not believe in the divinity of his brother Jesus until *after* His resurrection from the dead. We read in John 7:5, *". . . for even his brothers did not believe in him."* That is something that has made many of us wonder. The very brother of Jesus not believing in Him? It seems impossible! Harry Kemp has put it wistfully, in thought-provoking verse:

Joses, the brother of Jesus, plodded from day to day
With never a vision within him to glorify his clay;
Joses, the brother of Jesus, was one with the heavy clod,
But Christ was the soul of rapture, and soared, like a lark, with God.
Joses, the brother of Jesus, was only a worker in wood,
And he never could see the glory that Jesus, his brother, could.

. . . .

For he never walked with the prophets in God's great garden of bliss—
And of all the mistakes of the ages, the saddest, methinks, was this
To have had such a brother as Jesus, to speak with Him day by day,
But never to catch the vision which glorified His clay.

> —Harry Kemp, "Joses the Brother of Jesus." By permission of the author.

But let us be fair with James. This inability on his part to believe in the divinity of Jesus would be a perfectly natural reaction, for more than one good reason. In spite of the faultless character of Jesus and His unusual accomplishments, James undoubtedly found it difficult to understand how, in a home as intimate and humble as theirs, a blood brother of the circle could be the divine Son of God. Intimacy does not always breed understanding. "Familiarity breeds contempt," and "a prophet is not without honor, save in his own country"—or "in his own household." It would not be the first time that greatness of soul was lost upon a family circle!

Familiarity might not have been the only reason. Perhaps there was jealousy, too.

And then examine closely the old Jewish concept of the coming of the Messiah; it was a coming to be accompanied by elegance, grandeur and celestial power. Compare that with the humility of Jesus' birth, with the complete simplicity of His life, and with the quiet power of His love. The Messianic concept was born in heaven; the simplicity and the love were demonstrated on earth—and between heaven and earth a great gulf is found.

James was a Jew, one of a devout Jewish family. Against the ancient Hebrew background, it is not surprising that he was unable to believe in the divinity of Jesus until after the glory of the Resurrection. But then he *did* believe; we can never forget that. He became the first bishop of the church at Jerusalem, and it was to him that the Christians of the day, prominent and obscure, leaders and followers, flocked for fellowship and counsel; it was to him, and not to Peter, that they gave the highest deference. In that Holy City James was called "The Just One," for he was then upright, devoted and strong. It was then that his knees became calloused in prayer. The day came when James *did* "catch the vision," and came to kneel at the feet of the Brother sent from God. And perhaps it was better for him to come that way, for then he was fully convinced.

What was it that most impressed James in the life of his Brother? If we are to take his own words in this Epistle seriously, it was the works his Brother wrought and the life He lived—after, of course, the overwhelming impression of the Resurrection. In the life of Jesus he saw not only a faith but a force. It was something more than theology; it was a demonstration.

Here was a faith that was workable, a philosophy that carried with it a life-changing force. Here was a practical way of living, a realistic power to match the problems of the day. James was deeply impressed with the fact that through his Brother came a faith that stood all tests. It worked in practice as well as in theory —and James was deeply concerned with practicality. Dr. J. B. Phillips says, "Paul has said that a man is 'justified' not by achievement but by a real faith.

James says that the test of a real faith is whether it issues in appropriate behaviour." It is a good distinction.

All of us are interested in the practice of the Christian faith; it is the proof of the pudding. You and your family, I and mine, want to know whether or not this Christian faith is *workable*. In this book, we shall try to answer that question and to sum up the practical aspects of our faith in a consideration of certain questions asked and answered by James in his Epistle. The questions are:

    I. *How Do You Face Life's Trials?*
   II. *Is Your Religion Words or Works?*
  III. *Are You Prejudiced?*
  IV. *Is Your Tongue Converted?*
   V. *Do You Own a Peaceful Heart?*
  VI. *Are You Conceited?*
 VII. *Is Your Money Converted?*
VIII. *Can Your Faith Heal?*
  IX. *Are You a Soul Winner?*

If you can answer these questions in the proper way after your study of the Letter of James, then your brothers and your family may catch the vision of the divine Brother, too; your business associates will blink their eyes in surprise; your friends in the social whirl will begin to ask questions about you; and many a doubting Thomas may be arrested by the evidences of your life, filled as it can be with workable, practical power.

Living as we do in a day in which history wants to get at the facts, when philosophy is looking for corroborating experiences, and when contemporary psychology is everywhere studying the effects of belief on behavior, it is vital that we possess such a workable religion.

The chapters following, under the guidance of James, will press these questions upon our lives and minds. May we all find the unspeakable and thrilling experience of discovering within ourselves the affirmative answer: "It works!"

Make Your

Faith Work

When all kinds of trials and temptations crowd into your lives, my brothers, don't resent them as intruders, but welcome them as friends! Realise that they come to test your faith and to produce in you the quality of endurance. But let the process go on until that endurance is fully developed, and you will find you have become men of mature character with the right sort of independence. And if, in the process, any of you does not know how to meet any particular problem he has only to ask God— Who gives generously to all men without making them feel foolish or guilty—and he may be quite sure that the necessary wisdom will be given him. But he must ask in sincere faith without secret doubts as to whether he really wants God's help or not. The man who trusts God, but with inward reservations, is like a wave of the sea, carried forward by the wind one moment and driven back the next. That sort of man cannot hope to receive anything from God, and the life of a man of divided loyalty will reveal instability at every turn.

The man who patiently endures the temptations and trials that come to him is the truly happy man. For once his testing is complete he will receive the crown of life which the Lord has promised to all who love Him.

A man must not say when he is tempted, "God is tempting me." For God has no dealings with evil, and does not Himself tempt anyone. No, a man's temptation is due to the pull of his own inward desires, which can be enormously attractive. His own desire takes hold of him, and that produces sin. And sin in the long run means death—make no mistake about that, brothers of mine!

(James 1:2-8;12-15)

J. B. Phillips, in *Letters to Young Churches, A Translation of the New Testament Epistles.* Copyright 1947, and used by permission of The Macmillan Company.

CHAPTER I

How Do You Face Life's Trials?

The Letter of James starts out with this counsel: *"Count it all joy, my brethren, when you meet various trials, for you know that the testing of your faith produces steadfastness"* (James 1:2-3).

Count it all joy! Be happy about *everything* that happens to you! It is startling, and it is also an outstanding characteristic of the Christian faith, which dares to make such breathtaking, outlandish suggestions about our attitudes toward life's trials and suffering.

Even without God and Christ we may be joyful about *some* things—about good health, wealth, friendship, success, praise and security, for instance. That's easy. It takes no strong personality or great faith to feel joyful about the brighter aspects of life. But to be joyous, or thankful, about *everything*, to take that admonition and make it cover every tear, every fear, all fullness and emptiness, all disease and good health, all heartache and failure, all treasons, forsakings, disappointments and sorrows—*that* is faith in long trousers. All else is faith in knickerbockers.

Note that it is not just *endurance* of trial and tribulation of which James speaks. Many do that bravely, almost instinctively. James says that the endurance of trials and tribulation should be accompanied by happiness and rejoicing. "In everything, give thanks." "Rejoice, and again I say, rejoice." "Blessed (to be congratulated) are you when men revile you and persecute you and say all manner of evil against you falsely for my sake. Rejoice and be exceeding glad," said Jesus. It was Paul who said, "I glory in mine infirmities," and Peter who held that ". . . suffering is more precious than fine gold," and James is echoing all of them when he bids us to "Count it all joy . . . when you meet various trials. . . ."

So—at least to the founding fathers of Christianity —their religion equipped them with a joyous acceptance of affliction. It should do that for us, and it can, if we follow their thought.

The words "trials" and "temptations," in the Greek, do not mean so much the inner, heart-buried trials, but the external buffetings and pressures of life. James addresses his Epistle to a Jewish people who were feeling, at the moment, these buffetings and pressures. It was addressed to a people without a country, and living in foreign lands, to "the twelve tribes which are of the Dispersion"—or, as Phillips puts it, "to The Twelve Displaced Tribes" (James 1:1).

Those of the Dispersion were those in captivity, in slavery. Israel and Judah had been taken captive; they had been torn away from friends and country; they had suffered all the indignities of a conquered people. They were starving, homesick, the most loathed of men. Under the heel of the pagan conqueror, it would be natural for them to cry out, "Where is God?" James writes to tell them!

Now there were three captivities under this historic Jewish Dispersion. First, there was the one in Babylon, where they hanged their harps on the willow trees and sat them down to weep, and where they withstood the fiery furnace of Nebuchadnezzar. (We have a terrible modern parallel in the dispersed Jews withstanding the horrors of the concentration camps of World War II.) Second, there was the Syrian captivity, when they lay crushed under the gleaming shields and bright lances of the enemy, who were the Nazis of their day. Third, there was the Egyptian captivity, when they were forced to make bricks without straw.

For two hundred years these people had been scattered abroad as the prophets had warned they would be: "But every land is full of thee . . . aye, and every ocean." The Epistle of James, therefore, was written to people who suffered. It was written to demonstrate that Christianity, as James knew it, is a metal that can withstand the fires of adversity; it is a rock that withstands the erosion of storm and tempest and wear. Christianity is no hothouse faith. It is not an opiate for the beaten and the fearful: it is a cure, and a power. It is not a faith that holds firm only when there are no pressures; rather it is a faith that holds us steady in spite of the trials that come like tempests against us.

How do we gain such a philosophy of rejoicing in the face of pain and tribulation? Let us follow James, as he points the way.

He reminds us, first of all, that there are two varieties of troubles and trials: those we bring on ourselves, and those that come to us through no fault of our own. The King James, or Authorized Version translates it, "When ye *fall* into divers temptations . . ." (James 1:2). He does not say, "When we *walk* into diverse temptations. . . ." Sometimes we do walk into them with our eyes wide open, and then it is altogether our own fault that we suffer. Such trials are the result of our own sins, our own follies, our own selfishness, greed, malice or weakness.

Let's face it: many of our trials incubate in our own waywardness. James stresses this in the thirteenth, fourteenth and fifteenth verses of the first chapter of his Epistle, when he says that God tempts no man but that each is lured and enticed of his own desire. And this desire, when it has "conceived," gives birth to sin; and sin, when it is full grown, "bringeth forth death." Selfish desire plays a terrible role in our lives; we are lured by it and led on by it. When we have conceived it, tossed it about in our minds, thought about it *and planned it,* then sin is born. We forge the links of small compromising actions and before we know it, a mighty chain is wound around us and we are helpless.

And, full grown, "it bringeth forth death." That is the trouble! We nourish it, protect it, encourage it, allow it to grow within our hearts; then comes the day when, like a Frankenstein, it is stronger than we are, and it gets the best of us. Finally, it pins our shoulders to the mat—and we are completely whipped. I do not wrestle with my two full-grown sons any more; they are too big, and I know they would pin my shoulders. The same with sin, when we allow it to grow so within us, when we fail to rid ourselves of it. Sin grows tall—taller than we are! This is the origin of the thing we call "habit." That word starts with the Latin verb meaning "I have it." It ends with a vastly different connotation—"It has me!"

Yes, many of our trials and tribulations are the result of our own folly; God is not to blame for them.

But do not misunderstand me—or James. Our Christian religion has an answer and a remedy even for the trials which are self-created. Even when our own lusts are involved, there is pardon for that "fall." We have help when we are ready to turn around from the wrong we have walked with, and walk the other way. Even when we have defied God so wilfully, God has much to say to us and to do for us. For, if this whole area of self-inflicted suffering were to be placed beyond the realm of faith, if faith could not teach and help us there, then we would wander helplessly, hopelessly, through one of life's major areas—and God never lets any of us wander beyond His reach.

"Blessed," says James, "is the man that endureth temptation . . ." (A.V.). He is but echoing the Master's "Blessed are they which are persecuted for righteousness' sake. . . ." But what is *blessed* about it? What are these rich rewards which are promised to the sufferers, as God holds them within His reach?

First of all, trials are sent for the development of our characters. Read James 1:4: ". . . But let the process go on until . . . you have become men of mature character . . ." (Phillips). The King James Version puts it: "But let patience have her perfect work, that ye may be perfect and entire, wanting nothing." And Jesus: "Be ye perfect, even as your Father in heaven is perfect." That, of course, is the aim of our lives. Our character needs working over, developing, improving to a more perfect state.

The smith pounds temper into the steel; he subjects it to fire and pounds it upon an anvil. We do not say that the smith is cruel when he does that; it is the only way to fit that steel to our use, and to make it strong. God, the Smith of your character, must subject you to the fire at times, to the anvil of pain, to the poundings and buffeting of life, in order to temper your character

[24]

against the tests of tomorrow. He has a way of placing an oak, not in a hothouse where it will be protected, but out on the windswept hill where the winds may strengthen its branches and its roots. God grows ferns only in the shade, not in the sun. Do you suppose the fern objects to that, longing for the sun? There are flowers that grow and open beautifully in the shadows; there are others that need the sun. God knows, and acts accordingly! He develops the graces of character in us by placing us where He knows they will develop. Those graces are attained only through the trying experiences—in the shadows, more than in the sun of life.

Secondly, James tells us, these trials produce in us a quality of endurance—or steadfastness, or *patience* (James 1:3). This word "patience" comes from two words in the Latin: "patior," which means "I suffer," and "sensio," which means "with sense." That is, we face suffering sensibly. This is a patience that we will never learn until we practice it.

When a football coach wants to build a good team, he does not send it out on the field to play with soft pillows; he puts it to work against rough opponents, a bucking frame, a tackling dummy, and he puts it through exercises that are strenuous. God does the same thing with us, to give us the strengths of steadfastness and patience in our character: He marches us at times against tough opponents, against temptation, against public opinion, against discouragement.

Again, certain fruits are produced *only* under the stroke of severity. Apples do not grow where there is no frost. There are no clouds on the Sahara desert—and neither are there any flowers; tears are quite important in the horticulture of the spirit, as rain is important in the growing of flowers. There are, says Paul in Galatians 5, certain "fruits of the Spirit" which come like flowers nourished so. There is love—and that comes by practice, and if you do not practice it, you become unlovely. There is joy—which comes in spite of everything, every storm, every pain, every suffering. There is long-suffering, and you never achieve that virtue unless you suffer long. Gentleness is another fruit; it is the spirit of serenity with which you learn to accept the problems of life. Meekness—that is a fruit which might better be called "not kicking over the traces." And there is self-control, or a refusal to give way emotionally to the strains that are placed upon you.

Such are the fruits, the rewards of the Spirit. You may or may not think them important; that depends upon whether or not you want to grow in grace and in character. But keep this clear: it is certainly important to those who study you, who watch your life, who search it for that "workability" of the Spirit which they want in their own lives. It is important to those whose faith can be influenced by yours. For people do not trust God until they discover others who have learned to trust Him. They do not venture out on an untried faith nor accept an untried religion.

When a passenger plane takes to the skies, the passengers do not enter it until they see certain numbers and letters painted on the wings; those numbers and letters are put there only after the plane has passed the vigorous tests of flying under adverse conditions. So with your friends, with those who study religion. They must see you in the crash dives of life. They must be sure that the cantilever construction of your faith holds up; they must see you plunge into the abyss of great disappointment and level off for a smooth three-point landing, in conquering faith. They must be sure that the instruments of faith and trust permit you to "fly blind" through the fogs of life when the sun is hidden, when all is dark and the light has gone out of your sky.

A certain man stood looking at a beautiful white statue called "Faith." He was deeply impressed by its lines, its realism and its beauty. The next day he brought his family in to see it, but much to his surprise he found the statue melted down on its stand, reduced to a shapeless heap. What had happened? During the night there had been a rainstorm, and the rain had seeped through the roof and dripped upon the statue —which was made not of white marble but of white soap. The family stared at it in disappointment and in the disillusionment of a great deceit.

People are watching your life. Is it a life composed

of soapy sentiment, which will melt under the dripping of tears? Or is it made out of the granite of a confidence in the goodness of God, which stands firm and steady in the storm?

A church member, newly widowed, stood at the graveside of her husband; she screamed with uncontrolled and thoughtless emotion. A woman who knew her turned away in disgust, muttering, "Poor soul; I thought she believed it!"

Contrast this with the superintendent of a church school and his wife, who on Good Friday buried their two daughters, both dead of diptheria. No one expected them to be at their posts in the school on Easter Sunday—but they were there, he leading the hymns with a choke in his voice and she teaching her class through her tears. One of the boys in her class, walking home with his father from the class session, said, "Daddy, they sure believe it, don't they?" His father asked, "Believe what, son?" "Oh, all this about Easter and eternal life." The father answered, "Why of course, son. All Christians believe that." But the boy replied, "I know. But they don't believe it like *that*."

Do you believe it like that? When death comes, do you believe it like that?

If we are to exert a positive influence upon others in the realm of faith, we must call back to them, as we have come through our vales of tears, that Christ kept us to the end. They will be willing to experiment only on the basis of our experience. They will try it themselves only when *we* have triumphed. Their feet will not take them where we have not gone.

A poet with a great faith has written:

If you have gone on a little way ahead of me, call back—
'Twill cheer my heart, and help my feet along the stony track;
And if, perchance, faith's light is dim, because the oil is low,
Your call will guide my lagging course as wearily I go.

Call back—and tell me that He went with you into the storm;
Call back—and say He kept you when the forest's roots were torn;
That when the heavens thundered and the earthquake shook the hill,
He bore you up and held you where the air was very still.

O friend, call back and tell me, for I cannot see your face;
They say it glows with triumph, and your feet bound in the race.
But there are mists between us, and my spirit eyes are dim;
I cannot see the glory, though I long for word from Him.

But if you'll say He heard you when your prayer was but a cry,
And if you'll say He saw you through the night's sin-darkened sky—
If you have gone a little way ahead, O friend, call back—

*'Twill cheer my heart and help my feet along the
stony track.*
—From *Christian Work*

Once you have accepted this philosophy, do not
vacillate. Be constant and continued in your trust in
God. The prayer of faith is a mighty fortress. James,
with knees calloused from hours of prayer, found his
strength there. If you kneel to God today, you will be
able to stand up to anything tomorrow. Hold fast to
that unfailing principle of strength.

James advises us to ". . . ask God—Who gives generously to all men without making them feel foolish
or guilty . . ." (Phillips). Never feel foolish or guilty
when you pray; you are never so smart as when you
know your limitations; you are never stronger than
when you know you must lean on God.

Having committed your life to God, do not waver
between doubt and confidence. As Dr. Phillips translates verses six and seven, "The man who trusts God,
but with inward reservations, is like a wave of the
sea, carried forward by the wind one moment and
driven back the next. That sort of man cannot hope
to receive anything from God. . . ." We cannot say one
moment, "I want God's way," and the next, "I am not
sure that God leads me anywhere." The restlessness
of the tides of the sea is caused by the fact that they
are attracted upward by the moon and downward by
the gravity and silt of the ocean's bottom. The tides

simply cannot make up their minds which way to go! Let us not be tossed to and fro like that, because we cannot make up our minds as to whether or not we are the children of God. Don't forget that you have the assurance of divine support and strength from God sufficient for all your trials. Paul gives a companion promise to James', in I Corinthians 10:13: ". . . God is faithful, who will not suffer you to be tempted above that ye are able; but will with the temptation also make a way to escape, that ye may be able to bear it" (A.V.). The commercial trucks on our highways have their capacities stamped on their sides, in tons, hundred-weight and pounds. It indicates the safe load-limits of the trucks. You have a peak load, too, and God knows what it is. It is stamped on your personality, and if you are His child He will never allow any trial or temptation to press you down or break your spirit. If you have given your soul into the hand of God, trust Him!

There is one final, overwhelming reward waiting for you when you bear your trials courageously, happily and with faith: "Blessed is the man that endureth temptation; for when he is tried, he shall receive the crown of life, which the Lord hath promised to them that love him" (A.V.). This is the confidence and the reward of the long look. The Christian knows that the end of life is not a pile of ashes and a skull. It is this perspective that enables him to fashion a new standard of values. When Peter asked Christ, "We have forsaken all, and followed thee; what shall we have therefore?" he received a quick answer: ". . . every one that hath forsaken houses, or brethren, or sisters, or father, or mother, or wife, or children, or lands, for my name's sake, shall receive an hundredfold, and shall inherit everlasting life" (A.V.). We never gain a true sense of life's values until our souls take the long, long look.

A pastor spoke with a farmer—a member of his congregation—about his neglect in attending church. Said the farmer, "That is true, pastor, but I've been so busy sowing and harvesting, and I've had so little time for church. But I came out very well with my accounts, this November." To which the pastor replied, "That may be good, but remember, my friend—God does not settle His accounts in November."

Life with its failures and successes cannot be judged properly until a hundred years from now. Today you may be "keeping up with the Joneses," but is that a worthy goal for your life? Would you like to be where the Joneses will be a century from now? Is that life? Is that accomplishment? Is *that* the crown you want?

". . . once his testing is complete he will receive the crown of life . . ." (James 1:12, Phillips). There is a rewarding day; remember that! You might not see it now, but men do not always get their just deserts this side of the grave. There is a future praise in heaven that more than makes up for the scoffings here. There is a suffering with Him here that makes it possible for

[32]

us to reign with Him up yonder. There are humiliations here for the sake of godliness that are counterbalanced by the exaltations of a great tomorrow. *One never sees the full picture of God until he takes the future into account.*

Don't, I beg you, merely hear the message but put it into practice. The man who simply hears and does nothing about it is like a man catching the reflection of his own face in a mirror. He sees himself, it is true, but he goes on with whatever he was doing without the slightest recollection of what sort of person he saw in the mirror.

Religion that is pure and genuine in the sight of God the Father will show itself by such things as visiting orphans and widows in their distress and keeping oneself uncontaminated by the world.

(James 1:22-24,27)
Phillips' Translation

CHAPTER II

Is Your Religion Words or Works?

The sound of trumpets is in James 1:22: "But be ye doers of the word, and not hearers only, deceiving your own selves" (A.V.).

Jesus was good with words; He could preach. He painted pictures of the love of God and the fury of sin with a silver tongue; He lashed at men with His dialectic, and He soothed them with His comforts. He praised good men, and struck hard at the Pharisees. He held men spellbound in the amphitheatre of His Father's hills. Great were His words: ". . . the words that I speak unto you, they are spirit, and they are life" (A.V.). Men stood judged by His words, enthralled by them, chastised by them, encouraged by them, enlightened by them.

But what a worker He was! He was tireless. He healed all manner of diseases. Something happened wherever He went: people were transformed, homes were changed, a new spirit appeared in the market place, women were lifted to a high estate and children, loved as never before, became the patterns of the Kingdom.

Do you recall John the Baptist in Herod's prison, trying to figure out whether or not this Jesus was really the Messiah? He asked for a sign, or for signs, that Jesus was "He that should come," and Jesus sent word to him that "The blind receive their sight, and the lame walk, the lepers are cleansed, and the deaf hear, the dead are raised up, and the poor have the gospel preached to them" (A.V.). That settled the matter for John. His prison fetters would be lighter because of his enlivened faith in the Man he followed —the Man who proved His power with His works.

Always attending the *witness* of the apostles were the *works* their Master wrought in them. Here was religion in action. The disciples "went out, the Lord working in them." The old Hebrew faith, changed and electrified, sprang into action. The Greek mind really began to march after Jesus played His influence upon it: the two Gregories, Chrysostom, Origen and Justin Martyr rose as intellectual giants under His magic touch. They had the unanswerable credentials of a workable faith. There came the time when there was no room in the early church for those who were wordy without action; there is no room for them in the church of today.

In James 1:27 we read, "Pure religion and undefiled before God and the Father is this. To visit the fatherless and widows in their affliction, and to keep himself unspotted from the world" (A.V.). Here are two great essential facets of our Christian experience. May I have license to reverse their order? First, the Christian is to keep himself unstained, or unspotted, from the world. The clean life, the surrendered life, the life washed spotless with the blood of the Lamb, is of vast importance. But cleanliness must be followed by kindliness, which James saw exemplified in concern for the orphan and the widow. One follows the other, as the night the day; it *must*, if it is to be the faith of Christ.

A woman of considerable social and financial standing was visiting a tenement with a social worker. As they walked up the street, a filthy little urchin, clad in rags, tugged at her skirts. Pulling away in horror, she said to her companion, "How *dirty!* Doesn't the mother of this child love him?" To which the social worker replied, "Yes, the mother probably loves him. But you see, she just doesn't hate dirt. It works both ways. Some other mothers hate dirt—and do not love children."

Some Christians are clean enough, but they are not kind. Jesus discovered a woman taken in adultery; the scribes and the Pharisees were ready to stone her to death. Their hearts were as cold and unfriendly as the stones they held in their hands. Strong on "purity" and weak in "pardon," they loved to act as the prosecuting attorneys of humanity. The merciful kindliness and pity of the Lord sent them away with their heads hanging in shame. The faith that James saw in this Brother and which he embraced for himself was both righteous *and* merciful.

James also saw in Jesus a fine balance between hearing and doing. In James 1:23,24 we read: "For if any be a hearer of the word, and not a doer, he is like unto a man beholding his natural face in a glass; For he beholdeth himself, and goeth his way, and straightway forgetteth what manner of man he was" (A.V.). Or, as Dr. Phillips translates it, "Don't, I beg you, merely hear the message but put it into practice. For the man who simply hears and does nothing about it is like a man catching the reflection of his own face in a mirror. He sees himself, it is true, but he goes on with whatever he is doing without the slightest recollection of what sort of person he saw in the mirror." What laggards we are, seeing and hearing and doing nothing! We deceive ourselves but not God when we behave like that.

We suffer today from a "spectator complex"—watching, but doing nothing. We see a play and we are deeply disturbed; we weep a little, clench our fists at the wrong or the injustice walking the stage—and then go home and forget it! We feel without acting.

Let's put it in the church. On the gridiron of life, the church is playing its game against stubborn opposition—against the well-coached teams of low public morals, materialism and selfishness. In the stands sit the nonchurchmen, criticizing the churchmen, giving a Bronx cheer when the church is thrown for a loss, yet never offering to put on a suit and shoulder pads and get in the game, never offering to help the team of God on the field. They belong to the great "Association of Onlookers," those who talk and shout but will not work. Theirs is a comprehension without ensuing change.

There are two tasks for the preacher in the modern church: one is to reveal God to man and the other is to reveal man to himself. Sermons and devotional life ought to result in our holding up before ourselves the mirror of revelation. These functions of the Christian life, together with prayer and supplication, ought to enable us to see ourselves as we really are.

A woman, it is said, suspected her husband of unfaithfulness. One day she saw him put something into a barrel filled with sawdust. When he had left the house, she ran to the barrel and pulled out the hidden object; blowing off the sawdust and not realizing that she was looking into a mirror, she exclaimed, "So that's the old witch he's going with!" Few of us see ourselves as we are.

It is so easy for us to sit in a comfortable pew, listen to the sermon and immediately put up an umbrella so that the admonitions run down the other fellow's neck.

[41]

It is possible for us to hear a sermon on stewardship and nod our heads—and keep our purses shut tighter than tight. So many of us applaud the principles of the Sermon on the Mount—and live as though we had never heard of it. Someone has said that we boast on Sunday that we are the children of God, and live the rest of the week as though we were orphans. It has always been easier to fill the church with hearers than with doers.

The pity of it is that Christianity can work, *does* work, when we care enough about it to put it to work. We have only to look around us to see the spiritually lame walking, the spiritually poor made rich in the gospel, the spiritually blind given eyes. A Hindu and a Mohammedan and a Christian were discussing the relative merits of the three religions; they readily agreed on the presence of high ideals in each of the three faiths. "But," said the Hindu, "Christianity seems to be the only religion that gives its devotees the power to live out what they believe." If a Hindu feels that, what should we feel?

Unless the words written or spoken in a doctrine or a religion can manifest themselves clearly in the deed, there is no place for the doctrine or the religion in the lives of men. A watch, no matter how expensively put together, is a useless gadget without a mainspring. No matter how beautifully put together a religion may be, with all its lovely words and decorative ethics and philosophy—without the mainspring of a spiritual force to make it function it will never be used by men.

In this sense the laymen are really the preachers of our hour, since they are the practitioners. One dynamic minister gave this explanation of his over-crowded pews on Sunday: "I preach the gospel on Sunday, and my members live it all week long." Fortunate, able preacher! It is compelling, inasmuch as the best preaching is life lived after the Master's pattern, and this, in the church, lies as much if not more in the power of its members as in the power of its ministers.

Said Edgar A. Guest:

I'd rather see a sermon than hear one, any day;
I'd rather one should walk with me than merely tell
*   the way;*
The eye's a better pupil and more willing than the ear.
Fine counsel is confusing, but example's always clear,
And the best of all the preachers are the men who live
*   their creeds,*
For to see good put in action is what everybody needs.

I soon can learn to do it if you'll let me see it done;
I can watch your hands in action, but your tongue too
*   fast may run.*
And the lecture you deliver may be very wise and true,
But I'd rather get my lessons by observing what you do.
For I might misunderstand you and the high advice
*   you give,*

[43]

But there's no misunderstanding how you act and how you live.

—"Sermons We See," from the book *Collected Verse* by Edgar A. Guest, Copyright 1934, The Reilly & Lee Co., Chicago.

Don't ever attempt, my brothers, to combine snobbery with faith in our Lord Jesus Christ! Suppose one man comes into your meeting well dressed and with a gold ring on his finger, and another man, obviously poor, arrives in shabby clothes. If you pay special attention to the well-dressed man by saying, "Please sit here—it's an excellent seat,"—and say to the poor man, "You stand over there, please, or if you must sit, sit on the floor," doesn't that prove that you are making class-distinctions in your mind, and setting yourself up to assess a man's quality?—a very bad thing. For do notice, my brothers, that God chose poor men, whose only riches were their faith, and made them heirs to the Kingdom promised to those who love Him. And if you behave as I have suggested, it is the poor man that you are insulting. Look around you. Isn't it the rich who are always trying to "boss" you, isn't it the rich who drag you into litigation? Isn't it usually the rich who blaspheme the glorious Name by which you are known?

If you obey the royal Law, expressed by the Scripture, "Thou shalt love thy neighbor as thyself" all is well. But once you allow any invidious distinctions to creep in, you are sinning, you have broken God's law. Remember that a man who keeps the whole Law but for a single exception is none the less a Law-breaker. The One Who said, "Thou shalt not commit adultery," also said, "Thou shalt do no murder." If you were to keep clear of adultery but were to murder a man you would have become a breaker of God's whole Law.

(James 2:1-11)
Phillips' Translation

CHAPTER III

Are You Prejudiced?

It is trite but it is true: if you and I are born again and thus become people of the new life, we must *live* the new life. We will not have to advertise it; it will manifest itself. From the moment of the second birth we become creatures of a certain new type and demeanor.

Paul makes this demand of us clear in II Corinthians 5:17: "Therefore, if any one is in Christ, he is a new creation; the old has passed away, behold, the new has come." New attitudes have displaced old ones; new standards of judgment have replaced old standards; new relationships with our fellow men displace the old relationships. It follows, logically, that the new life will find itself thrillingly operative in our attitudes. "As a man thinketh in his heart, so is he"; his thoughts will be the basis of his new action.

It is clear, first of all, that in the very act of our adoption into the family of God, our relationship with God is changed. He becomes our Father, and we call

Him "Abba"—which means "Father" in a sense of nearness. It is the first new relationship of the new life. The old enmity is gone, and the estrangement of man from God is no more; being made one with Christ, we become as loving, understanding children of the Father. This is the first great thing that happens when we come to believe: "But as many as received him, to them gave he power to become the sons of God, even to them that believe on his name" (A.V.).

The second new relationship that develops in the new life is our relationship with others. All who enter into the new relationship with the Father enter into a new relationship with men. They become brothers and sisters in the faith. It is impossible to have the right attitude toward God unless we have this new, right attitude toward our human fellows. "By this shall all men know that ye are my disciples, if ye have love one to another" (A.V.). These two have now become inseparable: the Fatherhood of God and the Brotherhood of Man. The one is firmly linked to the other: if the Brotherhood of Man is not working in our lives, then the Fatherhood of God is not functioning properly in our hearts.

Notice now how all this goes to work—particularly on our unworthy prejudices. The true born-again Christian will make an early effort to beat down those prejudices, to drive them out of his life. In the Authorized Version, the words of James 2:1 are translated:

"My brethren, have not the faith of our Lord Jesus Christ, the Lord of glory, with respect of persons." On the face of it, this "have *not* the faith of Christ" seems to be an awkward translation. What could this possibly mean? It is better explained, I think, in Phillips' translation: "Don't ever attempt, my brothers, to combine snobbery with faith in our Lord Jesus Christ!" For prejudice (snobbery) can no more mix with faith than oil can with water. They are in complete antithesis. The humility of the process whereby you and I were adopted into the family of God, the very gift of grace whereby you and I were permitted to enter into God's family by faith—a privilege which He offers to *every* man—makes it impossible for us to be arrogant to others, if we really understand what has happened.

It will be impossible, first of all, to have prejudice on the basis of *possessions*. "Suppose one man comes into your meeting well dressed and with a gold ring on his finger, and another man, obviously poor, arrives in shabby clothes. If you pay special attention to the well-dressed man by saying, 'Please sit here—it's an excellent seat,' and say to the poor man, 'You stand over there, please, or if you must sit, sit on the floor,' doesn't that prove that you are making class-distinctions in your mind, and setting yourselves up to assess a man's quality?—a very bad thing" (Phillips). James puts his finger on a very sore spot. Money—which is affluence—has always stood for worth in the minds

[49]

of some people. Sometimes it *is* worth—when those who have it have come by it justly and honestly. It is possible, you know, for a rich man to gain his riches justly and honorably. "Seek ye first the Kingdom of God, and all these things shall be added unto you" (A.V.). That is a promise. Some men—let's admit it —*do* come into prosperity by first seeking the Kingdom. Some have been "diligent in business, serving the Lord."

You and I have no right to be prejudiced against a man merely because he is a man of means. Christ became King of Kings and Lord of Lords amid the sumptuous riches of heaven; then He emptied Himself and took on the form of a servant, for our sakes becoming poor. He was just and regal in both capacities—in His riches and in His poverty. George Washington, born to a noble family, became the father of his country. Abraham Lincoln, born in abject poverty, became the rescuer of the Union. History has learned to judge a man not by what he *has,* but by what he *is.*

But some of us still insist upon maintaining our prejudices against those who are financially prosperous. We adopt a "soak the rich" attitude, which is unchristian. "The ground of a certain rich man brought forth plentifully"—and Jesus did not condemn the man for that! It was in the man's favor that he made the best of his land. Some men strike the ground with

[50]

industry, and it smiles back at them with produce. The Master does not condemn them. He never condemned riches or rich men for the reason that they were riches or rich men, but only when they had allowed the accumulation of riches to become a low passion which drove out of their lives all worthier passions—including faith and action in the Fatherhood of God and the Brotherhood of Man. He had praise *for* the man who had five talents and in industry added five talents more. He also praised the two-talent man for doubling what he had while he chastised the one-talent man for *not* increasing what he had. After all, you cannot give unless you get, and I for one thank God for the people who have acquired, by the help of God, and who give unstintingly of their acquisition to the work of the Kingdom.

Let us remember that Christ was just as ready to use the rich as He was to use the poor in both companionship and cooperation in His Kingdom-building. Salome, the mother of Mark—whose rich gardens looked over Jerusalem and who is said to have owned the Garden of Gethsemane—was one of these. Certain women "ministered unto Him of their substance," and certain others kept His apostolic company from starvation as they went about teaching and preaching. James and John, of the firm of "Zebedee and Sons," owned their own boats and fishing equipment; they were not paupers. John is thought to have had considerable power in government and some influences among the princes of the realm. Nicodemus, His friend, was a ruler of the Jews. Joseph of Arimathea was a man of wealth. One of the military men who befriended Him was a centurion, with possessions sizable enough to enable him to erect a temple for his Christ. Jesus had no prejudice against riches, as riches; He only loathed the lustful desire for and foolish use of them.

Neither must we be prejudiced against the poor. Poverty is not necessarily a sin. Christ Himself knew poverty; He had nowhere to lay His head during a part of His earthly ministry. As far as we know, He had no bank account and owned no real estate. His disciples were far from rich—and they were often boycotted in the market place because of their allegiance to their penniless Prince. Paul lost practically everything but his soul.

You see, it is not a matter of what you have but of what you do with what you have. There were some Christians, in recent history, who found themselves in concentration camps because they had a stubborn, unconquerable faith and would not give it up. Following that faith, they fell from comparative prosperity to utter concentration-camp poverty. They didn't care about their riches; they cared only for their spiritual ideals. There are some who might criticize them for that, or at least feel that they were wrong in so choosing.

The world has one ideal, Christ and His followers another. There are some who deliberately choose those callings in life in which they cannot become rich. The pugilist, knocking his opponent unconscious, will be better paid for that than the schoolteacher who is trying to bring a higher consciousness to the human mind. The dance band leader will get ten times the salary of the choir director who arms the souls of people with a marching song. Those who erect buildings for big business will often be better paid than those who build temples of faith in the hearts of youth.

But keep it clear that the widow's mite received as much honor in the eyes of Jesus as the gift of the centurion who fashioned a temple for Him. We are judged not by the fullness of our possessions but by the faithfulness with which we handle them.

Jesus was ready to use the poor for a peculiar function of their own: in the realm of personal friendship, and in the building of a spiritual fellowship within the Kingdom. Read James 2:5: "Listen, my beloved brethren. Has not God chosen those who are poor in the world to be rich in faith and heirs of the Kingdom which he has promised to those who love him?" His choice of friends and officials in His Kingdom proved Him quite oblivious to either riches or poverty. Some of those who followed Him were fishermen, with worn garments; one was that poor widow who with her two mites bound herself to His heart with immortal memory. Lepers and blind men who had exhausted all their savings for a cure and found none came to Him with nothing in their hands—and He came to them with healing in His hands. Paul, once a man of affluence, emptied himself and came to the moment when he sat alone in a prison cell with only one friend—Luke, the doctor—at his side. Paul's only possession then was an old coat, but he was rich forever in heavenly things. After his beheading he entered the Kingdom of heaven to inherit heavenly, eternal riches, while Nero and his bloated demagogues languished forever in the darkness and poverty of Christ's rejection.

If our Christianity is working, we will number among our friends both the rich and the poor—both the haves and the have-nots.

James brought his examination of prejudice into the church; wherever he found it within the walls of the sanctuary, it received his chastisement. He would find much to chastise in our modern churches, I fear. Think, for instance, of the "pew rent" system which we had for so many years. The peril of that system of renting pews lay in the fact that it classified men; it gave them their seats in the House of God according to what they had, not what they were. It could become, and often did become, a matter of seating people on the basis of cash rather than character. Most churches have done away with this system of false evaluation. The story of an incident in one church which only recently abolished pew rents illustrates my point when I say it should be abolished everywhere. On the first Sunday when the pews were all "free," a woman of wealth and high social standing came up to her pastor after the service, during which an unkempt and somewhat unwashed person had sat beside her in the pew. "Pastor," she said haughtily, "did you detect an unusual odor this morning?" "Yes, madame, I did. It was the odor of sanctity." How right he was!

But when all is said, it seems to me that the church is winning its battle against prejudice based on money. I can honestly say that I cannot remember a single case, in any of my pastorates, where money was an object of worship among my church officials. That is true in most churches. Nominating committees are choosing men and women more for their abilities, their characters and spirits, than for their bank balances. Of course, many wealthy people hold prominent church positions—for the simple reason that they have proven themselves able and astute, in both secular and spiritual business; they have drive and vision, they are capable, successful and wise, and the church would be remiss if it failed to use them.

On the other hand there are many working in the officialdom of the church who carry no weight at all on Wall Street. Our Sessions and Official Boards are largely made up of tradesmen, doctors, lawyers, laborers and people from all walks of life. I look back on the completely unprejudiced official family elected in one church of which I was pastor; it included a chicken-rancher, a banker, a jeweler, a mortician, a janitor, a surgeon, a financier, an orange grower, a schoolteacher, a man retired and on pension, a horse breeder, a school superintendent, a dentist, a tree-sprayer and a carpenter. These men, *all* sons of God, were a happy, inseparable family; all were chosen for their abilities as leaders in the temple, and not for their social or financial affluence or lack of it. That is exactly as it should be; our religion should, must, dissolve prejudice based on possessions.

If our Christianity is working, we should also see the abolition from our lives of *prejudice in regard to sin.* James says, in 2:9-11: "But if you show partiality, you commit sin, and are convicted by the law as transgressors. For whoever keeps the whole law but fails in one point has become guilty of all of it. For he who said, 'Do not commit adultry,' said also , 'Do not kill.' If you do not commit adultry but do kill, you have become a transgressor of the law." It is possible for us to become prejudiced against certain sins and to be lenient with other sins. Perhaps you are not impure—but are you stingy? What did you put in the collection plate last Sunday? It is said that "Thou shalt not steal"; it is possible to steal by giving less than we should.

A Sunday school teacher asked a little girl, "What

is conscience?" The girl replied, "Conscience is something inside me that hurts me when my brother, Tom, does wrong." It is a common idea. The sins of others wound us more than our own—which means that we have turned prejudice in our own favor.

But sin is sin in any garb; God is no respecter of persons. The man who "pulls a fast one" in the stock market is no better than the man who steals milk bottles from the porch of a poverty-stricken tenement. A man in a tuxedo, sprawled drunk on a Persian rug, is not a bit better than the drunkard on Skid Row. The woman who walks the Bowery is no worse than the woman in the fine limousine who is thoughtless of God, the church and the Kingdom. The lazy woman who lives on charity because she is listless and slothful is the same sort of person as she who clips coupons and never lifts her hand in work for God or humanity. People who forget God in week ends of paganism, on a public beach or aboard a yacht, are guilty of the same sin. Those who sleep on a Sunday—in a mansion or a tenement room or a public park—are equally forgetful of God and His goodness. The man who could afford to give a million and gives a half million is just as guilty of covetousness as the man who gives fifty cents when he could give a dollar.

Paul was as ready to accuse Festus and Agrippa, in their royal robes, as he was to chastise the profligates in the street. Christ stormed at the money-changers in the temple court with the same vigor that He used against the beggars at the city gates. His barrage against the Pharisees was as devastating as the one against the thief who ran with the bag under his arm. Beneath the false, superficial garb of station, rank, class, position and social standing, He got at the heart of things. Men look upon the outward appearance, but He looked upon the heart. He knew what was *in* men. He had no prejudice regarding sin.

James warns us also against *prejudice based on race.* I thank God that He did, for I see that the seat of much of our trouble lies in our ethnological conceits. The races have thrown the world into chaos as they have boasted of their racial superiorities, be they white, brown, yellow, red or black; we have seen the shambles created by them as they have struggled to prove that racial superiority, and to force the world to live on their own racial pattern. Such a sociological pyramid will fall; it cannot stand on its apex. Civilization *must* be built upon the broad base of love and understanding.

Look back at the awful record! How many of our wars have come out of this stubborn and unfounded pride of race? In the time of the Caesars, the man without Roman citizenship had few rights and little standing. Alexander of Greece vowed that the world would speak Greek, think Greek and live Greek, since the Greeks, he said, were "the superior race." And then there was Hitler. At one time or another, nearly every race under the sun has been guilty of this sin of superiority.

We of today need to be constantly on guard against the insidious idea that the Anglo-Saxons are superior to all others. "God is no respecter of persons," in the matter of blood, for He has ". . . made of one blood all nations of men for to dwell on the face of the earth" (A.V.). No one of those nations steps on any other nation without suffering for its arrogance. England stepped on the American colonies—and lost them. France's royalty stepped on the poor—and came the Revolution! Germany crushed the Jewish people—and look at Germany now! Babylon persecuted Israel—and fell at the hands of the Persians. Turkey persecuted the Armenians—and became a mediocre nation. In the end, the proud and the arrogant are abased, both individually and collectively. Jesus never judged a nation by *whence it came,* but by *whither it was going.*

No man is responsible for his inheritance, but he is responsible for his direction. Whence he came means less than whither he goes. Ancestors are of some importance, but let us not overemphasize the accident of heredity. Should heredity have been of first importance, then Christ should have been ashamed of his family heritage; in His lineage was Rahab the harlot. But He never bowed His head because of that. Mary, the mother of Jesus, had her home in Nazareth, one of the most immoral little towns in Asia Minor; in Nazareth the caravans halted, and the rough camel-drivers made the nights hideous with their stupid, drunken voices. Yet in this environment Mary "walked with God." Let no man or woman say, "My town did this to me." Jesus grew up in the same town, as a lowly carpenter's son; some sneered at this, as though there was something bad about a man who made his living with hammer, saw and plane. But

Christ walked the same high road, and He bore the selfsame load,
When the Carpenter of Nazareth made common things for God.

No one would build his house within a thousand yards of the home of a tanner of hides in that day—but Jesus ate with Simon the tanner. He sat out in the broiling sun talking with a Samaritan woman, a woman whose blood was supposed to be polluted and evil because her forefathers had intermarried with the Assyrian conquerors. It was a sick, sad world—and Jesus moved through it like a shining Light.

It is a sick world in which we live—sick with the horrible illness of racial prejudice, of consciousness of class, station and possessions. It needs a Physician, and His name is Jesus Christ. The old order is still full of conceits, strife, pride, arrogance and disunity. The paper of humanity will fold again and again into the

same old creases unless, somehow, it is made into a
new sheet. "If any man be in Christ, he is a new
creature. . . ." We need a new understanding of the
Brotherhood of Man, and this will come to us only by
the power of Christ's regeneration. It is a *personal*
matter; society will be changed only *individual by
individual*.

Some time ago, Dr. Ivan Lee Holt said:

*I have been an enthusiast for the social gospel. For
years I have boasted my freedom in proclaiming that
message, and I do not believe that anyone has been
more moved by it. But my pastoral experience in recent
years has brought to me some of the conclusions which
his philosophy and experience have brought to Reinhold
Niebuhr. . . . The question I have been asking myself is
this: "Have I been as anxious about changed men as
changed environment?" I do not think of the efforts
for redeemed men and redeemed society as hostile to
each other. Now I make the statement, conscious of
both needs; once I made it and forgot the needs of
man's redemption. There is a need for an emphasis
where we have not been placing it in twenty-five years.*

*Let's be honest, as I am trying to be. Has it not been
easier to be noisy about some social injustice than to
get right on with the Bible and prayer and come to a
knowledge of God and Christ—the only Ones who can
change men or things?*

*Some of the most superficial thinking in the world
is about social problems as indicated by some daring
pronouncement—"I would rather go to jail than go to*

[61]

war"—as though that were getting at the roots of the matter!

We get out petitions against the mistreatment of Jews and negroes, but deep down in our hearts we never loved them—and we never will, until God changes our hearts.

With every social program must go a personal discovery of God, but we are too lazy to dig down into our own hearts to be sure we have it, and so the sands and the floods wash it away.

—Ivan Lee Holt, "The Return of Spring to Man's Soul," from *Harper Monthly Pulpit.*

We can build a new society, a new brotherhood, only upon the rocks of regenerated hearts. Our cry must be directed to God: "Create in me a clean heart, O God; and renew a right spirit within me" (A.V.). It must begin with *me.*

Does our religion work? James did not believe in the divinity of his Brother until he saw Him as the great conqueror of prejudices—loving the poor, eating with publicans, defeating class conceit wherever He found it, dining in the house of Simon the tanner to defeat prejudice in trade, talking to a Samaritan woman to the defeat of prejudice of blood, using the gardens of a rich woman to defeat the prejudice against wealth, walking with the poor to defeat the prejudice against those who were in want, walking with kings to defeat the prejudice against power and position, visiting with those in prison to defeat the prejudice against those who had neither freedom nor power.

So Christ walked, on this earth and in the hearts of men after He had left this earth. "How shall two walk together unless they be agreed?" They shall walk with *Him.* Do you?

We all make mistakes in all kinds of ways, but the man who can claim that he never says the wrong thing can consider himself perfect, for if he can control his tongue he can control every other part of his personality! Men control the movements of a large animal like the horse with a tiny bit placed in its mouth. And in the case of ships, for all their size and the momentum they have with a strong wind behind them, a very small rudder controls their course according to the helmsman's wishes. The human tongue is physically small, but what tremendous effects it can boast of! A whole forest can be set ablaze by a tiny spark of fire, and the tongue is as dangerous as any fire with vast potentialities for evil. It can poison the whole body, it can make the whole of life a blazing hell.

Beast, birds, reptiles and all kinds of sea-creatures can be, and in fact are, tamed by man, but no one can tame the human tongue. It is an evil always liable to break out, and the poison it spreads is deadly. We use the tongue to bless our Father, God, and we use the same tongue to curse our fellowmen, who are all created in God's likeness. Blessing and curses come out of the same mouth—surely, my brothers, this is the sort of thing that never ought to happen! Have you ever known a spring to give sweet and bitter water simultaneously? Have you ever seen a fig-tree with a crop of olives, or seen figs growing on a vine? It is just as impossible for

[65]

Make Your Faith Work

a spring to give fresh and salt water at the same time.
Are there some wise and understanding men among
you? Then your lives will be an example of the
humility that is born of true wisdom.

(James 3:1-13)
Phillips' Translation

CHAPTER IV

Is Your Tongue Converted?

Christianity is a way—a way of thinking, acting, feeling and *speaking*. No man is a Christian who has not given his lips and his speech to God; no man is truly converted until his tongue is converted.

James, in this Epistle, puts special emphasis upon failure to control the tongue; the amount of space he gives to the discussion is impressive. He admits that we all make mistakes (3:1), in "all kinds of ways"; and he remarks almost facetiously that "the man who can claim that he never says the wrong thing can consider himself perfect, for if he can control his tongue he can control every other part of his personality" (Phillips). Few of us can lay claim to perfection on the basis of such tongue control; rare is the man who *never* says the wrong thing! And the reverse of James' statement is true: if a man have a *loose* tongue, he may be loose everywhere, for that wagging tongue signifies a lack of central control in his personality.

Suppose we analyze with James the strategy, the

power and the importance of controlling the tongue. He says in 3:3 that "If we put bits into the mouths of horses that they may obey us, we guide their whole bodies." A few ounces of steel in the bit control half a ton of muscle, sinew and horse-power. And he has another illustration concerning ships, in 3:4: "Look at the ships also; though they are so great and are driven by strong winds, they are guided by a very small rudder wherever the will of the pilot directs." The leviathans of the sea are guided by comparatively tiny rudders.

What a guiding, influential instrument the tongue can be! A single speech in a senate can fasten a statute on a nation; a single phrase in one senator's speech can force the bill through. Armies have won victories with a single thrilling battle cry. Cromwell's Ironsides sang *Old Hundredth* and their enemies quailed before them. Mary Queen of Scots said of John Knox that she was more afraid of his tongue than of an army of 10,000 men.

Read more; read James 3:5,6: "So the tongue is a little member and boasts of great things. How great a forest is set ablaze by a small fire! And the tongue is a fire. The tongue is an unrighteous world among our members, staining the whole body, setting on fire the cycle of nature, and set on fire by hell." It is so easy to start a fire. Throw a cigarette into dry brush, and a forest flames to total destruction.

And what an inflammable instrument the tongue can be! One careless word tossed out of your mouth—and there is fire. One lie, one sentence of gossip with the lift of an eyebrow, one hellish insinuation, one evil story—and the conflagration begins. Human hearts can be like tinder, dry of the milk of human kindness and parched from lack of the rains of mercy; in such tinder the holocaust comes quickly, leaping through hearts and homes, across towns, into newspaper columns and conversations, fanned by the winds of hatred and man's merciless depravity, until the smell of burned flesh, destroyed homes and scarred souls is everywhere—all because one tongue wagged out of control. "How great a fire a little matter kindleth!"

Not only can the tongue inflame; it can act as a deadly poison. It is, according to James 3:8, ". . . a restless evil, full of deadly poison." Like a poisonous viper, it can strike without warning, and in a few moments a reputation is dead. It has a paralyzing effect, and it often slays the spirit.

The body of a woman suicide was pulled out of a river. Pinned on her coat was a piece of paper upon which she had written just two words: "They said!" It was enough. How many hearts have been broken, how many lives destroyed by the subtle intrigue of the human tongue?

A snake strikes without warning, and from out of sight, and then steals away in the grass to hide. There

[69]

is little use trying to run down the gossipers who, like vipers, crawl off in the concealing social grass, out of sight. They are hard to find. Now and then they can be tracked down and stepped on, but not often. Their poison does its work with startling speed.

All this is important in the church, where we have a fellowship which is, or should be, the stubborn enemy of the sin of the loose tongue. We have a wonderful unity in the church—or should have, for "we are members, one of another." Weymouth translates this, "We are *organs*, one of another." Whatever one says in the church affects all the other members—just as a poisoned finger or tooth can affect the whole human body. So it is of prime importance that as Christians and churchmen, we learn to control our tongues. It will have a salutary effect upon those outside the church who suffer from the same sin.

Now there are three fundamental laws concerning the Christian's conversation, and everything we say should pass through the net of these laws, or through these three screening processes. First, *is it true?* What proof do you have of it? Is there another side to the story, and did you consider it, carefully, before you spoke? It was said of one woman that she had "a keen sense of rumor." Of another that "To tell her anything is to put it on blotting paper—immediately it becomes both inverted and enlarged." There are those who say, as they gossip before they think, "Where there is smoke

[70]

there is fire." But that is not always true. His enemies said of Christ that He was "a winebibber and a glutton," that He made Himself a king against Caesar, that He was guilty of blasphemy, that He was starting an insurrection among the people. Here was "smoke"—but Christ was never guilty of such incendiary wrong, and even his tongue-loose enemies knew it.

The second screening test is: *is it necessary?* Do you *have* to say it? Why? You say you believe it is *true;* suppose God told everything about you that He knows to be true—would that please you? Is it the best thing you can say? Or do you want to tell it because it lies festering and swollen within your soul? Revenge and lovelessness are like pus sacs, sometimes, always ready to burst and paining when they do.

The third test is: *is it kind?* Will it dry tears? Or will it set tears flowing? Will it make hearts glad or sorrowful? Will it help or hinder in the service of God? Will it dampen a conflagration or spread its devastating effects? Is it something a lover would say?

If you are tempted to reveal a tale someone to you has told
About another—make it pass, before you speak, these three gates of gold:
These narrow gates: first, "Is it true?"
Then, "Is it needful?"—In your mind give truthful answers.
The next is last and narrowest: "Is it kind?"

And if, to reach your lips at last, it passes through
these gateways three,
Then you may tell the tale, nor fear what the results of
speech may be.

—"The Arabian." Author unknown.

Another offense of the unconverted tongue is that of cursing or blaspheming. James wonders how it can be, in 3:10,11, that "From the same mouth come blessing and cursing. My brethren, this ought not to be so. Does a spring pour forth from the same opening fresh water and brackish?" Of course not. And nothing evil ever issued forth from a man in speech which was not first resident in his spirit as either "fresh or brackish." That is why our speech is so revealing as to what is inside.

Today, cursing seems to be a "respectable" sin; but with all this false respect it is shocking and offensive to a Christian to have Christ's name irreverently thrown about from tongues that are disgusting in the ears of God. Why should a man choose the name of the most perfect character that ever drew breath to use it as an expletive, as a symbol of his uncontrollable temper or spiritual degeneracy? What good is there in cursing? It is painfully apparent that there is no good at all and much evil in it. Swearing often indicates a scanty vocabulary, a lack of sufficient words for proper expression. It also indicates a lack of reverence for all that is good. It is ill-bred and uncouth and it denotes a disregard for the feelings of others. It also condemns the curser, since ". . . (for) every idle word . . . they shall give account thereof in the day of judgment" (A.V.). It marks a man for what he is.

There are those who excuse their swearing and blasphemy on the ground that "it is just a habit." They have become unaware of their blasphemy. The worst thing that can be said of any of us is that we have lost all sensitivity to irreverence. When I was in Korea recently I saw lepers with fingers and toes rotted off by the horrible disease. I said to one of the doctors, "Their pain must be terrific." He replied, "No, there is little pain at this stage. The disease has gone too far." When cursing has become painless, when one is no longer sensitive to the irreverence that pours from his lips or from the lips of others, when he has lost that fine sensitivity that indicates an injury done to the deity, when the sin has gone so far that it is no longer accompanied by the pain of conscience—then the deadly malady is well on its way. All blasphemers, we are told in Holy Writ, "shall have their part in the second death." Blasphemy is not a trifling disease; it is a fatal malady.

"With it . . . we curse men, who are made in the likeness of God." So cursing men is actually cursing God. Hatred of men is hatred of God. These are the tenacious couplets of experience: love of man goes with love of God; hatred of man goes with hatred of God.

You cannot love one and hate the other; you either love or hate *both*.

With her arms around her father's neck, Mary was speaking words of endearment to him. But her mother noticed that over her father's shoulder she was sticking out her tongue at her brother Tom. The mother said, "Take your arms down from your father's neck, Mary; your father loves Tom as much as he loves you, and you can't stick out your tongue at your brother and love your father." When you hurl your curses, by word or deed, at those of another race or class, you must take your arms from around the neck of God.

There is no place in the life of the Christian for such tactics as Mary displayed—no place for the smears of a political campaign, no place for the innuendoes of a tongue-wagging theological dispute which can and often does reach the lowest ebb of spiritual honesty. It takes a long time for the truth to catch up with a lie, and meanwhile great harm is done; people are too quick to believe anything that is negative. Exercising control of our tongues today gives us less to do in restoring and making things right tomorrow. Certainly we have a right to speak out against evil, but this must be done *in love*.

Read again the words in James 3:10: "From the same mouth come blessing and cursing. My brethren, this ought not to be so." Of course it should not be, for no one can be two persons, one blessing and the other cursing. No spring, he further reminds us, can give water that is both fresh and brackish. Of course not! It gives out one or the other, but not both. When sulphur water comes from a spring, you know it is a sulphur spring. Alkaline water comes from an alkaline spring; there is no arguing that. Sweet water does not come from a bitter spring, nor sweet words from a sour soul!

A man was dining with a friend in a restaurant; the friend lost his temper and gave vent to a round of oaths. Hastily, he apologized with the words, "I'm sorry. I don't mean anything by these outbursts. Forgive me, please." The man replied, "Don't say you mean nothing by it. Watch this." He took a tumbler and filled it to the brim with water, carefully setting it down on the table. Then he clenched his fist and smashed it down on the table. Of course, water jumped out of the tumbler. Then he said, "Nothing splashed out of that glass that was not first inside it—and nothing comes out of your lips that is not first in your heart. Your speech is a dead giveaway, man. . . ." It is, and always will be. When we shout mean words it is because there is meanness within us.

Or there is James 3:12: "Can a fig tree, my brethren, yield olives, or a grapevine figs?" This is a fair criterion of judgment. The words that grow on the branches of conversation designate the type of tree. "No more can salt water yield fresh." The ocean always has its salty tang, and the world its own type of conversation.

It does no good to offer excuses; excuses are a dime a dozen, and worth less. Sometimes they are ridiculous, to say the least. "I swear before I know it, and I would stop it if I could." That says a lot for your weak mind and will, my friend! "I gossip, and I do say some awful things, but I don't mean to do so." Would you deliberately spread poison in your neighbor's rose garden, and then try to excuse it by saying you didn't mean to do it? "I lose my temper and go off like a machine gun, but it was not my deeper intention." How long since these baser surface intentions came into control of your life? "I know sometimes I say caustic things, but I say them without thinking." How long would you last at your job if you went at it without thinking? "I would stop it if I could." Have you really tried to stop it, or are you bluffing with such a weak excuse? We fool nobody with such nonsense. You swear because you want to swear; if you didn't want to, you'd stop it.

With such a malady of the tongue, certain curative steps are necessary. First of all, if you would stop this habit, *recognize that the trouble is deep within you,* and that out of the heart come the real issues of life. A man was having trouble with his watch. He took the hands off the watch and brought them to a watch repairer, saying, "These hands need fixing; they don't tell the right time." The watch repairer smiled and replied, "Sam, go bring me the works of your watch; the trouble isn't with the hands. It's somewhere inside." There is no use bringing God your tongue; bring Him your heart.

The second thing to remember is that unless *you* do this, there is nothing *you* can do. There is no other chance of controlling your tongue. You may control a dog, a horse, your car, your plane, but you cannot control yourself until you control your heart, or let God control it. "Every kind of beast and bird . . . has been tamed by humankind, but no *human being* can tame the tongue. . . ." Only God can tame that. The tongue is too strong for you; you need His dynamic hand. There is no room in James for mere self-control; he calls for Christ-control. If you ever needed God anywhere, you need Him here, for He can do for you what you cannot do for yourself.

In the third place, *practice love and praise.* "Do good to them that hate you . . ." (A.V.). Practice loving your enemies. List them—and praise them at the first opportunity. You say, "That is not reasonable." God says it is! If you are using the therapy of the Spirit, you must listen to the Surgeon of the soul.

Practice praise; for one week make up your mind that only good will come from your lips. God will take care of the censure and the criticism which will come to you as you do it. For one week at least, trust Him with that retribution.

[77]

This will remove jealousy, too—for jealousy is something that can be removed by the affirmative practice of love. One man was very jealous of a merchant down the street who sold the same line of goods. But he conquered his jealousy and ill will by making up his mind that whenever he did not have something a customer asked for, he would suggest that the customer go to his competitor. It worked. He practiced love—and the jealousy disappeared.

In the fourth place, "Pray for them which despitefully use you" (A.V.). Prayer is a scalpel that lances the pus sacs of hatred; it is spiritually impossible to go on hating someone for whom you pray regularly and sincerely. Try it; it is one of the Spirit's greatest curatives.

Finally, put on a *campaign* for love, extending for more than a week. Every day let something good be said. Meet evil with goodness. Meet persecution with praise. Hatred never solved anything, and in the last few years we have all been poisoned with the spread of it across the world.

James Whitcomb Riley had it about right:

When over the fair fame of friend or foe
The shadow of disgrace shall fall; instead
Of words of blame, or proof of so and so,
Let something good be said.

No generous heart may vainly turn aside
In ways of sympathy; no soul so dead

But may awaken strong and glorified,
If something good be said.

And so I charge thee, by the thorny crown,
And by the Cross on which the Saviour bled,
And by your own soul's hope for fair renown:
Let something good be said.

One of our most tragic failures is our inability to control the spirit. Someone told of visiting Poet's Corner, in Westminster Abbey. Among the tombs of the great in this place are the tombs of some who could handle words, but who could never handle or control their spirits. "Drayton, the poet, sleeps a little way from Goldie, who said Drayton was not a poet. Dryden lies not far from Shadwell, who pursued him like a fiend. There also lies Pope, just a little way from Dennis, his implacable enemy. These men had never before come so close together without quarreling." They had received great applause for their abilities to bring words into rhyme, metre and harmony, but they could not get along with each other. They died, in a way, as paupers, in wretchedness of disposition. They never learned the one great harmony of life: how to get along with each other.

Shakespeare said that some men were "talkers, and not doers." Not that these men were any more guilty than you and I often are, but, as Raleigh warned, "He that is lavish in words is often a niggard in deed." It is up to us to prove this to be untrue in our own lives. Don't be a spendthrift with your tongue. Say what you mean, and let the meaning come from a cleansed heart.

It might help us to think of it all in terms of this prayer:

O Christ, a walk with Thee will make a difference. Our speech will betray us then; we shall come upon the dialect of heaven, and our accents of love will disclose the fact that we belong to another Country. A new life will give us a new vocabulary; our verbs will take on a new vitality of love, and a new spirit will captain our speech.

We shall acquire the habit of praise, and in every hour shall something good be said. All vehemence of speech shall then stem from our hatred of wrong, never of the evil-doer, and our words shall fall like a gentle rain from heaven upon a field of humanity parched for praise and for love.

In this holy trait, make us like our Lord today, more like the Master. With our heads raised to Thee in holy supplication, we plead for this miracle that will touch our tongues and change our speech. Work this miracle of the new life in us, O Christ. May the world see that our religion works, and having heard what falls from our lips, cry out, "Thou hast been with the Galilean —thy speech betrayeth thee!" Amen.

But if your heart is full of rivalry and bitter jealousy, then do not boast of your wisdom—don't deny the truth that you must recognise in your inmost heart.

For wherever you find jealousy and rivalry you also find disharmony and all other kinds of evil. The wisdom that comes from God is first utterly pure, then peace-loving, gentle, approachable, full of tolerant thoughts and kindly actions, with no breath of favouritism or hint of hypocrisy. And the wise are peace-makers who go on quietly sowing for a harvest of righteousness—in other people and in themselves.

But what about the feuds and struggles that exist among you—where do you suppose they come from? Can't you see that they arise from conflicting passions within yourselves? You crave for something and don't get it, you are jealous and envious of what others have got and you don't possess it yourselves. Consequently, in your exasperated frustration you struggle and fight with one another. You don't get what you want because you don't ask God for it. And when you do ask He doesn't give it to you, for you ask in quite the wrong spirit—you only want to satisfy your own desires.

(James 3:14,16-18;4:1-3)
Phillips' Translation

CHAPTER V

Do You Own a Peaceful Heart?

James asks an arresting question in 4:1: "What causes wars, and what causes fightings among you?" And he answers it in 3:14: "But if you have bitter jealousy and selfish ambition in your hearts, do not boast and be false to the truth."

Here is the plain truth: the explosive jealousy and selfish ambitions of the human heart can and have inspired wars large and small, individual and global.

So let our discussion in this chapter be both personal and collective. The question, "Do you own a peaceful heart?" has of course a definitely personal significance, inasmuch as the heart is personal. You and I were created, according to the Westminster Confession, to "glorify God and enjoy Him forever." That is a matter for the heart, and it calls for something more than casual consideration.

Evidently heaven is a place where we enjoy God forever, in company with a myriad of others. This means that we enjoy *them*, as well as the place called heaven. Heaven, then, is a place where people have learned to get along happily, to live in peace and accord with one another, to live in unity of spirit. It is peopled with folks such as you would wish to live with forever, with people whose faces you would be pleased to look upon eternally, whose company and conversation you would always enjoy. If this be true, then this life is a vestibule of eternity in which it is altogether necessary that our religion prepare us for whatever is ahead, by making of us such persons as could live happily with others through all time. Does our religion work like that?

Let's not dodge the issue by suggesting that "We shall all be changed in the twinkling of an eye." That is too often an excuse for going on in our miserable human state on the silly assurance that God will work a fast trick of magic when we die and change us into something clean and wholesome. That is shameful; it is laughing at Christ's command to obey His commandments while yet we live and move on this earth. You don't fool God with that one! As a matter of fact, this verse about our being changed has more to do with the body than with the soul. We shall have, after death, "a more glorious *body*," yes, but in the sense of the soul there is a sense in which death does not change the real you, which includes soul as well as body—a sense in which it merely "fixes" you. It makes you more and more what you are at the time of your death. John

[84]

speaks of it, in Revelation 22:11: ". . . he which is filthy, let him be filthy *still* . . ." (A.V.). The word "still" here means "more and more." ". . . he that is righteous, let him be righteous still . . ."—or more and more righteous, to the nth degree.

Death takes what you are and multiplies it, infinitely. If you are mean at death, you will be meaner and meaner thereafter. If you are kind, you will be more and more kindly through the ages. If you are peaceable, you will be more and more peaceable for eternity.

Christ said, "Blessed are the peacemakers, for they shall be called the children of God" (A.V.). And "He that hath not my spirit is not of me." It is impossible for us to qualify for peaceful fellowship with God unless we have learned the art of peaceful fellowship with men. Christ is the Prince of Peace, and you and I must come to love His peace, and to own within ourselves His peaceful heart.

Now, let us come back to the question in 4:1: "What causes wars, and what causes fightings among you?" What is the origin of a cantankerous disposition? How does it incubate, and what causes it? What brings about friction in the home? A young man in the army said to one of his buddies in the front line, "Man, this sure is terrible, isn't it?" The other replied, "Boy, if you knew what my home was like, you'd know what a relief this is!"

In business, why the friction, the jealousy, the stab-

[85]

bing in the back? At the club, why the jealousy, the meanness, the petty hatreds? In the church, why the censure, the criticism, the unkindness, the disunity? James has the answers, in 3:14 and 3:16: "But if you have bitter jealousy . . . in your hearts . . . where jealousy and selfish ambition exist, there will be disorder and every vile practice."

It is here that we fail, in the human equation. No amount of instruction in the technologies will suffice unless human nature has learned to use the techniques of happiness rather than those of destruction. A Christian is one whose emotions have gone to school, and it is this sort of schooling of which we stand in desperate need.

For wars do not start by spontaneous combustion; they come to fruition when unspiritual attitudes wrangle in the human heart.

A storm is caused by hot air rising and cold air rushing in to take its place. Many storms in the social order —personal, national and international—have their origin in *a jealous desire for displacement;* in one desire or ambition rushing in to displace another. Politically, a candidate wants to unseat an incumbent, or one party wishes to replace another in power. On the football field, a man on the bench desires to replace a man in the line-up. On the stage, one actor wants another's part. In a business organization, one man runs another down in order to build himself up. Envy and jealousy are at work. We deprecate, we criticize, we undermine in order to establish ourselves. These subtle evils are also found, regretfully, in the church. But they can be conquered. I have heard of one clergyman who watched a pastor close by getting overflow crowds while his own church was only half filled; he said, in fine Christian spirit, "We will have room for his overflow in our sanctuary. And may God bless him." We could use more of that!

Jealousy can be displaced only when God is on center in our lives—when the cause for which we labor is greater than our personal ambitions.

Another cause of war and misunderstanding lies in *our desire to have*—in an unreasonable lust to acquire. "You desire and do not have; so you kill. And you covet and cannot obtain; so you fight and wage war." Behind most wars between nations and individuals is a passion to have and to hold. Property, money, prestige, power and position have become the storm centers of life.

Nations desire to have and they cannot obtain—so they fight to possess. Clemenceau once said, at a diplomatic conference, "If we want peace, then the British must get out of India; we French must get out of Indo-China; the Americans must get out of the Philippines." When the leaders of the nations remonstrated with him, he countered by saying, "Then it is not peace you want, but war!" And he was right, as subsequent events have proved. As long as the struggle in the family of nations is primarily one for balance of power and a jockeying for position, we cannot expect a lasting peace.

Insofar as war between nations is concerned, it is time we understood that in modern war everyone involved ends up empty handed. Nobody wins; it costs too much for both victor and vanquished. Someone painted a picture of "War," and in it depicted an old woman sitting on a rubble heap in a ruined city, unraveling the knitting she had done through two hundred years of war. She was the world.

War brings empty chairs, widows, orphans, scars, debts, bad memories, insane asylums, hospitals, rubble heaps, ships in mothballs, gold stars on service flags, broken homes, frustrated plans and disillusioned youth. Hatred never pays; nobody wins in war. It pays poor dividends. Every shell that explodes, every rocket that is fired, every battleship that is launched robs someone of God and bread. War is humanity hanging on a cross of iron, and we shall never be rid of these iron crosses until we lift high above them the cross of Christ with its power to change and regenerate the human heart.

But let us not lose ourselves in international generalities; there is an individual obligation here. Phillips translates James 4:2: "You crave for something and don't get it, you are jealous and envious of what others have got and you don't possess it yourselves. Consequently, in your exasperated frustration you struggle and fight with one another."

Now a tiny war can start as you sit in your chair, perhaps in a poorly furnished room, hating people who may be sitting in elegantly furnished surroundings listening to the same radio program, or reading God's Word as they hold it in well-manicured hands. It is possible for you right there to eat out your own heart with jealousy. Or from your workbench you glower at the "stuffed shirt" employer as he drives off in his new eight-cylinder car while you look forward to driving your battered old "six." The woman who wears a cloth coat becomes bitterly envious of another woman who goes about in furs.

Covetousness is a horrible thing, and it sometimes cuts deeply into the finest minds. The have-nots become violently aroused against the haves; the haves are jealous of the mass power of the have-nots, and fear their uprisings. People with salaries in four figures rise to smite those whose salaries run to five or six figures. Small churches criticize large ones, saying, "These big churches are not spiritual." Perhaps it is the smaller church which has lost its spirituality! Yes, covetousness is a terrible thing! It invades every avenue and circumstance of life.

But let us go on to the affirmative elements that make for peace. Just what elements lie within the wisdom that will help us do away with striving and war? James lists them.

First he says, ". . . wisdom from above is first *pure*." "Pure," in this case, means "unmixed in motive." We must seek first the Kingdom of God; this we must desire above all else. When we are sure of that, then self is not pursuing glory for itself but for the glory of Christ. This will make it impossible for us to strive and work for ourselves—for praise, glory or mere position. For us then, to live will be Christ.

Let the athlete ask himself this question: "Is it the victory for my school I most desire, or glory for myself?" Let the businessman ask, "Am I laboring for the success of my firm and my colleagues, or merely for my own advancement?" In the church, let the singer, the teacher, the officer ask, "Am I doing this for the glory of Christ, or for love of leadership and position?" This purity of motive is still far distant from too many of us, far even from some who name the name of Christ. Self is still enthroned; the abdication has been only a partial one. What can we truthfully say of the motive that guides our lives? How far along are we?

The next element that makes for peace is *gentleness*. "But the wisdom from above is . . . gentle. . . ." This is the gentleness that makes us great. The bravado that attends our actions at times is actually an inferiority complex asserting itself. The larger animals are usually less irritable than the smaller ones, although this is not without exception. They have about them a certain confidence that comes from strength; lacking that strength, the old inferiority complex asserts itself, and they become irritable. The irritability rises directly out of a sense of personal lack.

Again, this wisdom from above is "open to reason . . ." or, "easy to be entreated" (A.V.). We must be approachable; we must have about us a lovableness, a sense of understanding, a humility. We must not build a wall of aloofness around ourselves. Some men throw up an iron curtain around themselves; it is hard to get to them. They have put on an armor of separateness that separates them from the needs and approaches of others. It is difficult to reason with them; they are opinionated, and somehow you sense the fact that they feel more than they think.

"But this wisdom from above is . . . full of mercy and good fruits. . . ." *Full.* This mercy, these good fruits —or works—are not attained by a single act of philanthropy; they become the natural, *continuing* characteristics of the Christian. They become the spiritual habit that fuses all his conduct. Acts of kindness emanate from some people as naturally as oranges grow on an orange tree; they are the normal fruitage of loving hearts.

This wisdom "is full of tolerant thoughts and kindly actions . . ." (Phillips). That is, kindly *reactions*. It is the woman bringing a plate of hot buns to the neighbor who has gossiped about her. It is the man doing a favor for one who has stabbed him in the back. Someone said of Henry Ward Beecher, "If you want him to do you a favor, just kick him." Is this your reaction to enmity and wrong? If we do good only to those who do good to us, we are no better than the pagans, who also do that. They crucified Christ on a cross, but He did not call for crosses for them; He called out, "Father, forgive them; for they know not what they do" (A.V.). This forgiveness of Christ stands supreme in the realm of "kindly reaction."

This wisdom from above which brings peace is "without uncertainty"—or without *partiality*. It carries with it "no breath of favoritism"; it is able to get along with people no matter who they are—no matter how fat or lean their bank accounts, what clothes they wear, where they live, what the color of their skin. The Christian must strive to be as impartial as God. We have so many allergies, so many unfortunate and unjustifiable reactions against other races, for instance, that we need the injection of divine love to cure us.

The wisdom from above is "without insincerity," or, as Phillips translates it, "without hint of hypocrisy." We should be perfectly frank with ourselves and merciless in searching out our own sins and shortcomings. We should stop condemning in other people things which we are guilty of ourselves. Many of us burn up a lot of spiritual energy criticizing others while we refuse to fight the same sins in our own hearts. We Americans are particularly good at that.

We Americans are guilty of a good many nasty sins—broken homes, widespread divorce, juvenile delinquency, a murder every forty minutes. The list is long. And we are so quick to condemn the "criminal tendencies" of other countries! That reveals a lack of sincerity within the American heart; we place ourselves in the position of the woman who was asked why she had discharged her maid; the woman replied, indignantly, "Why, I caught her stealing my Waldorf-Astoria towels!"

The ways of peace are followed by people with a sharp sense of personal obligation, those who do their parts by *becoming peaceable persons.* Phillips translates James 3:18, "And the wise are peace-makers who go on quietly sowing for a harvest of righteousness— in other people *and in themselves.*" We must begin here; we must first sow the seeds of peace within ourselves. A forest is made up of thousands of trees; the peaceful community is made up of thousands of peaceful people. The flower garden is gorgeous in its total effect only because the separate blooms have taken on beauty and color.

On the other hand, a storm at sea is made up of thousands of tempestuous waves. If we contribute to the general chaos our own personal tempests, our own critical, censorious, intractable, proud, irascible dispositions, we shall be adding individually to the collective storm. We must ask ourselves frankly, "Lord, am I part of the problem, or a part of the solution?"

Once, just before I was to speak to a convention of student-body presidents at Pennsylvania State College, a young student came to me and said, "I prayed a prayer last night that was the hardest prayer of my life." I asked, "What was it?" He said, "I prayed, 'Almighty God, may I never ask Thee to do for the world what I have never allowed Thee to do for me.'" I said to him, "That *is* praying. It is the only way to pray."

Are you and I willing to say this today: "O Christ, I shall never ask Thee to do for the world, collectively, what first I have not allowed Thee to do for me?" This would bring peace.

Are there some wise and understanding men among you? Then your lives will be an example of the humility that is born of true wisdom. But if your heart is full of rivalry and bitter jealousy, then do not boast of your wisdom—don't deny the truth that you must recognise in your inmost heart. You may acquire a certain superficial wisdom, but it does not come from God—it comes from this world, from your own lower nature, even from the devil.

Come close to God and He will come close to you. Realise that you have sinned and get your hands clean again. Realise that you have been disloyal and get your hearts made true once more.

You will have to feel very small in the sight of God before He will set you on your feet once more.

Never pull each other to pieces, my brothers. If you do you are judging your brother and setting yourself up in the place of God's Law; you have become in fact a critic of the Law. Yet if you start to criticise the Law instead of obeying it you are setting yourself up as Judge, and there is only One Judge, the One Who gave the Law, to Whom belongs absolute power of life and death. How can you then be so silly as to imagine that you are your neighbour's judge?

(James 3:13-15;4:8,10-12)
Phillips' Translation

CHAPTER VI

Are You Conceited?

James is deeply concerned about conceit—with the conceit of riches, the conceit of power, the conceit of race, the conceit of class and the conceit of intellect or mind. The last conceit displays itself in judging others, in criticizing, condemning and ostracizing people; it has been responsible for too many heartaches in human society.

It starts with hauteur of mind, as James hints in 3:13: "Who is wise and understanding among you? By his good life let him show his works *in the meekness of wisdom.*" He is speaking of two types of wisdom here. He has just mentioned *the wisdom of living a good life,* but in the fourteenth and fifteenth verses of the same chapter he mentions the opposite—the wisdom that is *full of strife and envy. That* wisdom ". . . is not such as comes down from above, but is earthly, unspiritual, devilish." It is earthly because it is a most unheavenly thing to acquire. It is unspiritual because it is based on the most carnal motives. It is

[97]

devilish because devils love to use it. The devil is called Beelzebub—"the belittler of humanity."

This devilish wisdom comes from the Greek word "sophos," from which in turn comes our word "sophistication." It has to do with an assumed smartness or cleverness, a pretense which makes us judges when we are not qualified to judge. James strikes directly at this particular conceit in 4:12: ". . . But who are you that you judge your neighbor?"

This is the tragic conceit that leads a man to sit himself down on the bench beside God, that persuades him to put on the judicial robe and predicate to himself the wisdom to judge the rest of humanity. We have no such right. It is false, arrogant and detestable—and blasphemous.

But we must at the same time keep it clear that James speaks here of an *evil* form of judging and that he is not condemning *all* judging, per se. There is a justifiable judgment of conduct and attitude which is quite respectable. "By this shall all men know that ye are my disciples, if ye have love one to another"; or, "Whosoever hateth his brother is a murderer . . ." (A.V.). We *must* draw judgments in such matters as these.

We also have a right, or an obligation, to judge in matters of doctrine. I John 4:1 puts it: "Beloved, believe not every spirit, but try the spirits whether they are of God: because many false prophets are gone out into the world" (A.V.). John proceeds from this to give us certain criteria for the judgment of true as against false doctrine. Truth must be guarded, and James, like John does *not* advocate a flabby condescension to untruth. There are times when we, as Christians, must "serve in the courts of God." Just as jurors are called for duty in our secular courts of law, so should we expect to be called for duty in His holy courts. Protecting and upholding true doctrine as written in the Bible, we must be guided by love, imbued with kindness and motivated by truth. We have a right, too, to criticize a person dear to us, or to criticize the country we love, for the purpose of further ennobling that which we cherish.

But this brand of constructive reproval is a far cry from the nasty desire to hurt through criticism. James warns us against the love of finding fault. The Greek for this type of judging, in 4:11, is *katalalain,* which means harsh, censorious judging, or judging uncharitably, or invading the prerogatives of others. In situations where there is a possibility of two opinions, the wrong is in maintaining that yours is the only correct opinion. It is judging without adequate evidence (which might better be called prejudice) that is sin; it is sitting in the judgment seat where only God has a right to sit that is blasphemous. It is listening to rumors, misinterpreting the opinion or attitude of another, being unable to look into a neighbor's heart, having a critical, censorious attitude that is the antithesis of love, that is evil.

Let us analyze this conceit, with James. It arises, he says, out of a lack of humility within ourselves. (James 4:12: ". . . But who are you that you judge your neighbor?") What unusual characteristics do you have, what unique fund of knowledge and judgment is yours, that humanity should stand before you as you presume to sit with God in judgment?

Pride is the most subtle of all sins, and it comes to us in different forms. One of these is habitual fault-finding, which comes out of an unfounded assumption of superiority. We shout so easily, "Here I stand!", as though we were certain that unless everyone else stands exactly there, they are out of touch with God. We are terribly in error when we do that. We may be certain that we "fly the radio beam of God's will," but remember that a radio beam can be fifteen miles wide and that many planes fly wingtip to wingtip and are still on the same beam. There is a breadth of truth and interpretation which allows people to go along with us on the journey without always identifying themselves completely with our particular brand of opinion or interpretation.

In the realm of theology we must leave room for others in their interpretation of the Scriptures in such matters as baptism, eschatology, ethics, prophecy, etc. It is strange that many who are most critical of the theological attitudes of others are often those who are least erudite in knowledge of the Scriptures. One man said to me of another, "That man is a leftist." I replied, "My dear fellow, you are so far to the right that *anyone* who differs with you must be to the left." Some other people are so far to the left that everyone who differs with them is, in their opinion, "disgustingly to the right."

This narrowness creeps into the church. There are some people who believe in only one form of baptism simply because they steadfastly refuse to consider any other form. There are some who believe in only one kind of prophecy because all the books on prophecy which they have read are chosen, not to make them think, but simply to confirm their own prejudices in the matter. One minister said to another, "How many people attend your church on a Sunday morning?" "Eight hundred." "But I thought your church seated only four hundred people." "Well, my people are so narrow that they can sit two in one seat." It is possible to be just that limited—to narrow down our own peculiar interpretation of truth as *we* see it, and be blind to all else.

It is often evidenced in our denominational pride. You will remember that John once hurried to Jesus and said, "Master, we saw one casting out devils in thy name; and we forbade him . . ." (A.V.). Jesus made it plain to John that they had no right to forbid him, that there are different ways of casting out devils, and that all men were not obliged to conform to any one method of doing it. We should all realize, by this time, that there is no *one* way of casting out the demons. The Congregationalists reason them out; the Lutherans stay them out; the Pentecostalists shout them out; the Methodists sing them out; the Baptists drown them out—and the Presbyterians freeze them out! What does it matter, really, *so long as we get rid of the devils*? This conceit of method has harassed the church for too long; it is high time we conceded to each other a difference in method which is still well within the circle of God's will.

We see the same conceit in the political arena. There are those who come to such a horrible state of party conceit that they are no longer able to see anything good or even decent in the man who is of another party. They have looked so long through the smoked glasses of their own political prejudices that it is impossible for them to see virtue in anyone of different political opinion.

In business and industry, capital has long had the ignoble habit of believing itself to be always in the right, whatever the issue, and labor has succumbed to the same temptation. Only recently have labor and capital been able to sit down around the same table and at least try to understand each other and to plan for the welfare of both.

[102]

Conceit to James is *a usurpation of God's powers.* "There is one lawgiver and judge, he who is able to save and to destroy. . . ." God says, "Vengeance is mine; I will repay . . ." (A.V.). There are some judgments which we must leave to God. Pilate said to Jesus, ". . . Speaketh thou not unto me? knowest thou not that I have the power to crucify thee, and have the power to release thee?" (A.V.). To this Jesus replied, "Thou couldst have no power at all against me, except it were given thee from above . . ." (A.V.). God has the final power to judge, and *He alone.* The supremacy of the judgments of God in this universe must always predominate. He, at the end, is the sole font of authority, and He allows no man to share His judgment seat in the higher brackets of life. Do you have power to crucify and to release? Not at all—unless God in His wisdom has given you this power from above. As earthly beings, we have no right to crucify any individuals; no right to drive the nails of pain through their hands, to thrust the lance of unjust criticism into their sides, to hold them up on a cross of public censure and ridicule without just cause. God allows no man to assume His prerogatives. His judgment is upon us when we do.

Who are you to judge your neighbor? The evils of our neighbors are resident in us as well as in them. Is there that blamelessness in us, that purity of motive, that perfection, that overflowing charity, that love of the sinner that makes us like Christ and so qualifies us for unprejudiced judgment? James challenges us to a sense of humility in this whole area.

In Matthew 7:4,5, Christ asks us, frankly but kindly, this question: "Or how can you say to your brother, 'Let me take the speck out of your eye,' when there is the log in your own eye? You hypocrite, first take the log out of your own eye, and then you will see clearly to take the speck out of your brother's eye." Taking care of our own sins would keep us busy enough, and this personal cleansing will deliver us from the extreme sin of censuring others. Handling the defense in our own case before the judgment seat of God will keep us too busy to act as prosecuting attorney in bringing others to justice.

Wherein lies the cure for this conceit of judgment? A diagnosis without a cure is irritating, but James has the cure as well as the diagnosis. He says in 4:8: "Draw near to God, and he will draw near to you. . . ." In this nearness to God, the Great Physician, certain things will inevitably happen. There will be a process of cleansing; the verse continues: ". . . Cleanse your hands, you sinners, and purify your hearts, you men of double mind." It is in the heart that the cleansing must begin. James adds, in 4:10: "Humble yourselves before the Lord. . . ." There must come over us a sense of humility regarding our sins. We must begin with the Psalmist's "Create in me a clean heart. . . ." The cleansing must begin in *me*. God loves a broken and contrite heart—and until it is broken and contrite, it is not acceptable in His court of justice.

We must also receive a new baptism of love. A "right spirit" must be renewed within us. This love comes upon us with the experience of self-crucifixion. Too often, I think, we are more anxious to justify ourselves than to help our fellow man. Too often we want to win our argument, even though in winning it we lose our man. One day a clergyman wrote a stinging reply to a caustic criticism of himself which had appeared in the public press. He laid his reply before some friends with whom he was accustomed to discussing his problems, asking their opinion of it; they returned it to him with the words scrawled across it, "Not sufficiently redemptive." It did not make them think of Christ on Calvary. In his reply he had won his argument and lost his man. Self in him was still very much alive, and he had not yet been "crucified with Christ." It is difficult for most of us to be so crucified—to die to self and live unto Christ. "We know that we have passed from death unto life, *because we love the brethren . . .*" (A.V.). We must dethrone self, enthrone Christ—then only do we have the spirit of love.

A minister tells of two children who were good friends and who went to a church service together. Each wanted to sit beside one particular grown-up friend; one succeeded in pushing the other aside and getting the coveted seat for himself. The second one had to sit alone, in front. The victorious one smiled, elated at his triumph. Suddenly, however, he became very unhappy, realizing that he had obtained his own way at a price. He had satisfied himself, but he had lost a friend. He tried to change things, tickling the back of his friend's neck, but the friend paid no attention. There was only one way to make peace; he went up and sat beside the one he had displaced. A new person had gotten up from his seat—an unselfish person. A new friendship was formed in that moment —a friendship of love.

It must be like that with us. This humility, this abdication of self, must take hold of us, for only as we are so "crucified with Christ" do we begin to "live." I know of no other way in which we can come together in loving friendship than by "the upward tug of God" that will lift us to Himself. It is the way of love.

And now, you plutocrats, is the time for you to weep and moan because of the miseries in store for you! Your richest goods are ruined, your hoard of clothes is moth-eaten, your gold and silver are tarnished. Yes, their very tarnish will be the evidence of your wicked hoarding and you will shrink from them as if they were red-hot. You have made a fine pile in these last days, haven't you? But look, here is the pay of the reaper you hired and whom you cheated, and it is shouting out against you! And the cries of the other labourers you swindled is heard by the Lord of Hosts Himself. Yes, you have had a magnificent time on this earth, and have indulged yourselves to the full. You have picked out just what you wanted like soldiers looting after battle. You have condemned and ruined innocent men in your career, and they have been powerless to stop you.

But be patient, my brothers, as you wait for the Lord to come. Look at the farmer quietly awaiting his precious harvest. See how he has to possess his soul in patience till the land has had the early and late rains. So must you be patient, resting your hearts on the ultimate certainty. The Lord's coming is very near.

Don't make complaints against each other in the meantime, my brothers—you may be the one at fault yourself. The Judge Himself is already at the door.

(James 5:1-9)
Phillips' Translation

CHAPTER VII

Is Your Money Converted?

Three arrogances appear in the Epistle of James. The first is the arrogance of judging which we find so brilliantly outlined in his second chapter. The second is found in 4:13,15; the arrogance of planning without God: ". . . Today or tomorrow we will go into such and such a town and . . . trade . . . Instead you ought to say 'If the Lord wills . . . we shall do this or that.'" It is arrogance to put our wills above God's.

Then there is the third arrogance, which we now have under consideration: the arrogance which rises out of a wrong use of money, or out of the seeking, saving and spending of money without the benefit of God's counsel. This is the arrogance which forgets that God is the owner of all of life, not owner of part of it.

Is your money converted? It is said that a man about to be immersed exclaimed to the pastor who was about to "put him under," "Just a minute, pastor. I want to take my wallet out of my pocket." The minister replied, "No, my friend, leave it where it is; that

[109]

goes under, too!" It was good advice. Too many of us come up the church aisle singing "All to Jesus I surrender; I surrender all—*except* my pocketbook."

There is no such thing as partial conversion; either God has us in our entirety or He does not have us at all. To separate some things from the whole is to kill them. Subtract the carburetor from the engine and it becomes a mass of useless metal. Pluck the petals from a flower, one by one, and you destroy the beauty of the bloom. Amputate a part of the body—a leg, a hand, the mind, the heart—and you have either disfigurement or death.

Now money, in a sense, is a vital part of your personality. You made it; you earned it by the sweat of your brow; you accumulated it by the sacrifice of physical strength and energy, by the expenditure of your time and the application of your mind. And its acquisition did something to your *soul*. When an artist makes a statue, two things result from his work: the finished statue, and the dulling of his tools. So it is with the getting of money: the most important results lie in the amount we have made and the erosive effect upon the tools we have used to get it—the tools of conscience, disposition, vision and ideals.

We talk much of stewardship in the Christian church; we should always remember that stewardship involves not only man's way of making money, but also God's way of making men.

Money is important because it is still, in a sense, the barter medium of the Kingdom. Missions cannot operate without it. If the Bible is to be translated and given to the heathen, the American Bible Society must have funds. It is God's will that diseases be healed in His name—but that requires money for research, prevention and cure. Without medicines people die—and medicines cost money. Train up a child in the way he should go, yes—but the teachers must be paid. It is quite impossible to leave consideration of money out of any consideration of life.

Furthermore, love expresses itself, to a degree, in the expenditure of money. Look back in your Old Testament and see how God thought of that. He commanded the children of Israel to build a tabernacle for Him in the wilderness, and He gave most explicit instructions about that tabernacle. He wanted no stinting, no mean economizing here. The sockets on which the tabernacle was to be built were to be made of silver and planted in the desert sands. The Ark of the Covenant, with its Shekinah light symbolizing the presence of God in the tabernacle, was to be overlaid with fine gold. The covering of the tabernacle was to be of the most expensive materials: fine linen, and ramskin dyed red. Shittim and acacia wood, the finest in the land, were to be used. This was to be a magnificent thing, symbolizing the high regard in which the people held their God.

When the regard lessened and the temple was allowed to fall into disrepair, the people were still beaming the ceilings of their own houses with precious wood—a sight which filled Jesus with indignation. The temple decaying, and the houses resplendent: that He could not stand. Can you help but wonder what He must think of *us* as we build gleaming homes and give pennies to the church building fund? The church is to be as beautiful as "a bride adorned for her husband"—but is it? May He have mercy upon us for being niggardly in the construction of His house while we lavish money without stint upon our own dwellings!

There are always those who protest against anything that is even merely adequate in the way of church buildings, and who argue that the money would be better spent on missions or—à la Judas Iscariot—on the poor. Sometimes they may be right; undoubtedly there are some instances of exorbitant expenditure in church construction, but I wonder if this sort of criticism is not usually leveled at the church by those who, themselves, are men of miserly heart. Judas complained when the alabaster vase of ointment was broken over Jesus' feet, but his complaint was voiced not out of love of the poor but out of his own love of bag and money. Judas was covetous, selfish, and stingy. Some of us may consider these "respectable" sins, but they should remember that it was because of these sins that Judas went out and hanged himself. The

hardest man to convert is often the man whose money
has not been converted—the man who holds back his
purse.

It is clear as we read James' Epistle that there is
nothing in it which condemns the making of money;
its condemnations have to do with the *abuses* of money.
He is negative about riches only as he warns us against
the perils of unsurrendered, unconverted, undirected
money. First of all, he reminds us of the *inadequacy*
of riches. He never thought, as some of us seem to,
that money will do anything, buy everything. He had
heard Christ, his Brother, say that ". . . a man's life
consisteth not in the abundance of the things which
he possesseth" (A.V.). James echoes that sentiment
in the first verse of his fifth chapter: "Come now, you
rich, weep and howl for the miseries that are coming
upon you." He is pointing out the possibility that riches
and misery may visit a man together. He has something there!

Riches were never a cure for all that ails us, and
no man can make his life revolve satisfactorily around
what he possesses. Money does not automatically
bring happiness. Divorce seems to visit as many homes
in the higher salary brackets as in the lower. Sometimes
it seems that the more money people have, the more
they fight about it. A home cannot know happiness if
it revolves about the sun of financial sufficiency.

There is the wealthy woman, for instance, who was

visited by her pastor. He waited for her in a drawing room the walls of which were covered with costly paintings; there were rare tapestries, rich wall-to-wall carpets and expensive furniture. As she swept into the room he said, "How happy you must be, in such splendid surroundings." She responded by going quietly to a carved teakwood table, opening the drawer and taking out a pearl-handled revolver. "I would use this today to end it all," she said, "were it not for the embarrassment it would cause my dear ones and my friends." Teakwood tables, oil paintings and the tapestries of life cannot in themselves bring happiness. ". . . a man's life consisteth not in the abundance of the things which he possesseth." Miseries can spawn as easily in the midst of money as in the absence of it.

Our ways of *making* money must be converted. James says, "Your riches have *rotted*. . . ." That is, the soul had rotted in accumulation of gold and silver. He makes a serious charge against the manner in which certain money-makers have piled up their wealth when he says, "You have condemned, you have killed, the righteous man. . . ." Their way of making money was a ruthless, murderous way. They had oppressed less fortunate men; they had ground down the less able men under their greedy heels. They had fattened their hearts "in a day of slaughter." Don't condemn them too severely until you take a good look at yourself.

We are doing that, right now. We in America are

fattening our hearts—and our bank accounts—by contributing to the slaughter of widespread war. We do not all hate war, whatever we say; some of us love it, for it makes some of us rich. In time of war—and even in times of rumors of war—unemployment almost disappears as we go about forging the instruments of destruction in our shops and mills. Gigantic automobile factories are retooled to produce tanks and bombers; there is more money in that! Slaughter can be a very profitable business; war can mean wealth. The profits of war have made many pray for its return or continuance. And any economy that rests upon such a philosophy of slaughter is fundamentally rotten and evil. When we build upon it, we build upon shifting sand.

Of course, there are those who say blithely that "whatever is economically sound is morally right." But is it? Is that true, for instance, of the liquor traffic —which seems to be economically sound, since repeal? We brought liquor back because we thought that bringing it back would bring new revenue into the public treasury. But has it? The figures show that financial losses due to work stoppage because of inebriation, and the money spent on the building of institutions for alcoholics, far exceed the revenue realized from liquor sales. How stupid can we get? How cheaply do we sell our souls! Add to this more than half of the quarter-million people slaughtered every year on the highways in accidents involving drunken drivers or inebriated pedestrians—a far worse slaughter than that inflicted upon us by armed enemies—and you begin to get the picture in true focus.

It is so easy for us to nourish ourselves on slaughter! James saw it clearly, and he speaks in his Epistle to *every* industry that fattens itself on the murder of mankind. We must make our money in good conscience; it is a crime for any of us to be in any business that does not, as Roger Babson says, "make people healthier and happier."

James becomes painfully frank about certain "slaughter" practices in employer-labor relations: ". . . the wages of the laborers who mowed your fields, which you kept back by fraud, cry out; and the cries of the harvesters have reached the ears of the Lord of hosts. You have lived on the earth in luxury and in pleasure. . . ." He is speaking of an unjust sharing of profits. Some there are who think that this is not the business of religion, but only of economics. We must remember that as Christians *all* our actions must be built upon a cruciform foundation, and that our economics must rest upon the economics of the cross. James doesn't mince his words; he tells us plainly what God thinks about certain economic practices that are inherently selfish and unjust.

There is such a thing as a just and living wage; to pay anything less than that, James suggests, is unjust and sinful. Whether some of us like it or not, it is a

Christian as well as an economic principle that "the laborer is worthy of his hire," and that the worker should not be exploited and cheated by avaricious employers. There is such a thing as a "Christian economy" which must be worked out by the conscientious Christian employer under the generous laws of God.

But James, in this passage, is primarily interested in the use and disuse of money. He counsels against hoarding and greed: "Your gold and silver have rusted, and their rust will be evidence against you and will eat your flesh like fire. You have laid up treasure. . . ." I do not believe that James was condemning *saving* wealth, but that he was condemning *hoarding*. There is a perfectly justifiable manner in which we *should* save today to meet the demands of tomorrow, and for which none of us can be condemned. But there is also a compelling demand upon us to use what we have for God.

If you do not use the muscles of your body they will atrophy and wither away. If you do not use your mind it becomes stultified, stale and inert. If you do not exercise your soul in worship and praise, in love and action, it will shrivel. If you do not squeeze a sponge it hardens into rock. The tire that stands unused in the garage rots and deteriorates. Dust on the Bible means drought in the heart. An unused well becomes stagnant. An unused tool rusts. And money, left idle

[117]

when it might have been put to good use, corrodes and turns black, literally as well as figuratively. Have you noticed that those who collect coins are very careful to keep their coins from tarnishing? It is even more necessary for the Christian to keep tarnish from the soul when the coin of the Spirit is left unused—or when the coin of the realm is left idle when it might be working for God.

The best way to keep our money is to give it away. I think the obituaries in the newspapers make a great mistake when they tell us what a man is "worth" by telling us what he leaves behind him. He is worth only what he has given away—for that is what he takes with him! "Lay not up for yourselves treasure upon earth, where moth and rust corrupt, and where thieves break through and steal" (A.V.). You can't take it with you—but you can send it on ahead by spending it for spiritual purposes.

". . . your garments are moth-eaten," says James. As with money, so with clothes; disuse means ruin. Moths thrive in unused garments, and the moths of mercenary spirits thrive in treasure lying idle in the closets of unconcern. The accumulation of unused or scarcely used garments to be found in our American closets would clothe half of Europe. There is a "holding on" which leads to poverty.

Turn now to take the long look at all this, as James sees it: "You have laid up treasure *for the last days*."

[118]

The rich fool in Jesus' story did this; he laid up too much. With supreme confidence he looked at his bursting barns and the goods he had accumulated, and said to his soul, ". . . take your ease, eat, drink and be merry." He was not really addressing his soul, of course; he was speaking to his belly and his bank account. Then a Voice came saying, "This night thy soul shall be required of thee; then whose shall these things be, which thou hast provided?" (A.V.). It wasn't important that he happened to have all these things today; who was to have them *tomorrow?* With what shall you face the *last* days? How shortsighted, how slavish we are today! We are like the president of a huge business who bought a private railroad car and furnished it luxuriously; he wanted it just for the twenty-mile commuting trip between his home and his office! We are all on a longer trip than this—but we seem to be more ready to spend our money on the short haul than on the long one.

The last days! What are they? When do they come? There are differences of opinion here; some believe in one last day of gigantic catastrophe, others, in several last days of comparatively minor disaster. Perhaps we have already seen some of these days. When we spent our money like spendthrift fools on the weapons of destruction, we got in payment one horrible "last day" for Hiroshima. Whenever we spend more in our laboratories for education in brutality than we do in our churches on education for godliness and love, we get a bill due on the last day.

Peter warns us, in II Peter 3:10,11: "But the day of the Lord will come like a thief, and then the heavens will pass away with a loud noise, and the elements will be dissolved with fire, and the earth and the works that are upon it will be burned up. Since all these things are thus to be dissolved, what sort of person ought you to be in lives of holiness and godliness . . . !"

You say, "But God would not do that to the universe, and to us!" Perhaps not—but man might quite conceivably do it to man!

President Eisenhower said some time ago that what we need now is a regeneration of the Spirit throughout the world; that if we did not have it we might all go up in the dust of an atomic explosion—*and that all this meant a great chance for the church.* What a chance this is! Perhaps it is not so much a chance as a desperate necessity: unless we begin spending our money in regenerating man and disarming his hands instead of arming him with the tools of global suicide, we can and *may* all melt in fervent (atomic) heat. It happened at Hiroshima and it could happen again—anywhere!

A great scientist said some time ago to a college audience, "If we haven't learned to live together as Christian people within the next five years, we may all have died together." I am no prophet or son of a prophet, but I agree with the President and the scientist that the peril is real, and close. What good will all our money do us if, after the last atomic explosion on the last day, someone carves on our tombstone the words, "Here lies a *very* rich man!"? Riches have no significance at all once they are divorced from spiritual investment.

The best way to avoid this kind of "last days" is to invest in the spiritualities of the *present* day!

It has always been a moot question as to how much a Christian has a right to "lay up": the problem of saving and spending is a complex one, and we cannot arbitrarily settle it here. It is, however, hard to see how great accumulations of wealth can be defended in a day when missionary doors are being slammed shut all over the world for lack of funds to keep them open and when many are starving for lack of bread abroad while we have more than enough at home. The church goes begging to those who refuse to let their pocketbooks be tapped for such need. One wonders what sort of defense will be made by those who withhold from God when the time comes for the great accounting. How can anyone justify the hoarding of large sums that could be used magnificently in the advancement of the Kingdom of God? Or how does one justify stinting God with one's wealth and leaving it, at death, to an irresponsible progeny? One millionnaire has said, "I do not believe in leaving large sums to my children. If they need it, they have proven that they neither know how to make it nor to handle it. If they do not need it, there are others who do. I will not curse my children by leaving them great wealth." To which we can hear James cry, "Amen!"

There can be no separatism in our religion, or in our personalities. We are saved or lost not piecemeal but *en toto,* as a unit or not at all. We are either all Christian or not Christian at all. The statesman, Talleyrand, was a notorious liar, as a statesman; he would lie like a trooper to gain his ends, and excuse it all on the ground of "the end justifies the means." When a friend asked him how he could possibly call himself a Christian (which he did) and at the same time lie so frequently and easily, he replied, "I lie as a statesman, not as a Christian." The friend then replied, "When the statesman is in hell, what will become of the Christian?" Exactly! Apply that idea to a Christian and his money: how can you keep your money from God and expect God to accept *you?*

When money is given to God by man, it is, in a fashion, stamped with that man's name, "laid up in heaven" as a treasure against the last days. What a man has and is are a united dichotomy; they are, in a way, saved or lost together. God grant that as Christ watches us cast our money into His treasury He may know that our money is converted—that both cash and character are His, that both soul and silver may be under His sway, that our persons and our purses are altogether His.

One of our poets has pictured Jesus sitting "over against the treasury," watching the people "cast their money into the treasury," in these arresting lines:

Unnoted He sat by the temple gate
While the rich and the poor passed by;
And He read their hearts as they dropped their gifts
'Neath the gaze of His searching eye.

Each gift He weighed in a subtle scale
As it dropped in the temple store—
And the pain it cost, and the sacrifice,
And the burden of love it bore.

But the piercing eye of the watching Christ
Looked not at the proffered gold;
Not "What did he give?" was His searching test,
But "How much did he withhold?"

By that standard stern the rich man's tithe
Was shamed by the widow's mite;
For she gave her all—while he kept his wealth
As he passed from the Master's sight.

By the gates of the treasury still He sits,
And watches the gifts we bring—
And He measures the gold that we give to Him
By the gold to which we cling.

How much to revive a starving world?
How much for our pampered plates?

[123]

How much to extend the King's frontiers?
How much for our own estates?

How much have you sent to the mission field
To invest in the souls of men?
How much to your broker for stocks and bonds
To return to yourself again?

Is it Mammon or God who holds the key
To the vault where your treasure lies?
There's a curse or a blessing locked within
That will follow beyond the skies.

For the hour will come when the wealth of earth
Recedes from our slackened grasp;
And the gold and the goods we have given away
Are all that our hands can clasp.

Oh, Master of men, spur our lagging zeal
Till we answer the Kingdom's call,
And lay on the altar a worthy gift,
Ourselves and our gold, and all.
                    —F. C. Wellman, from *Meeting House.*

James closes this section of the Epistle with a word about patience—the patience of God and the patience of man. He uses the farmer as an illustration—the farmer who puts in his seed and waits patiently for God to bring the harvest. Man should model his patience on God's. How patient God is with us! He waits patiently for us to stop cheating Him with our miserly tithes and offerings. He waits patiently for

America to learn that it is not enough for America to give *two per cent* of its income to God and the Kingdom and who knows what per cent to Mars and war. In Caesar's time it cost seventy-five cents to kill an enemy soldier; in the Napoleonic Wars it cost $3,000; in our Civil War, $5,000; in World War I, $20,000; in World War II, $50,000. How patient we are with war, and how much more patient is God as we go from war to war! When will we learn its ghastly futility, when will we become so out of sympathy with it that we will begin to invest more heavily in the business of changing, converting the human heart instead of investing in armed suicide?

God still says, in His amazing patience, "Bring the *whole* tithe into the store-house." When we have done this He will open the windows of blessing and pour out upon us such a treasure of goodness that we shall not be able to contain it. This will be the result of the patience of God, and the result of our own converted stewardship.

The rich young ruler asked, "What good deed must I do, to have eternal life?" Christ put His hand on the young man's purse. That was not all the solution, but it was part of it, for the rich young ruler sinned greatly in holding back the contents of that purse. Christ told him that it was his failure to turn his purse over to God that was keeping him from eternal life and the Kingdom's gates. His pocketbook was not converted.

His morals were converted; he obeyed the law. His faith was good, for he came seeking to the Master. These were Christ's—but not his purse. That was his fatal lack.

Someone has said, "If I were a hymn, my prayer would be: 'Dear Lord, may I not be a third verse.'" For third verses are often sung dispiritedly, or omitted altogether. Take, for instance, the hymn which begins, "Take my life, and let it be Consecrated, Lord, to thee...." That's the first verse, and we sing it lustily. We begin to taper off a little when we come to the second verse, which begins, "Take my voice, and let me sing, Always, only, for my King." And a lot of us slow down to almost a dead stop when we come to "Take my silver and my gold; not a mite would I withhold...." That is important, whether we like it or not. It is proof of our faith.

As we sing our song of praise, may it include our silver and our gold! Else perhaps we had better not sing at all.

If any of you is in trouble let him pray. If anyone is flourishing let him sing praises to God. If anyone is ill, he should send for the Church elders. They should pray over him, anointing him with oil in the Lord's name. Believing prayer will save the sick man; the Lord will restore him and any sins he has committed will be forgiven. You should get into the habit of admitting your sins to each other, and praying for each other, so that if sickness comes to you you may be healed.

Tremendous power is made available through a good man's earnest prayer.

(James 5:13-16)
Phillips' Translation

CHAPTER VIII

Can Your Faith Heal?

Thus far, James has reminded us that God is a Judge and that as such He alone will judge the world; therefore we must not be so foolish or careless as to exercise prerogatives which belong to Him alone. He has said that God is a Father, and that as His children we must practice brotherhood with all men. He has shown us that God is the owner of all things, and that as such we must recognize His authority over our possessions. He has contended that God is the Ruler of the Universe; if He be such we must trust Him for the supreme guidance of our lives.

And now, in 5:13-16, James reminds us that God is also the Creator and Sustainer of our bodies; He has power to make and keep us healthy. Our failure to recognize this would indicate that we believe God and religion to be ruled out of that large part of man's life involved in his physical self; it would mean that the Christian faith, insofar as *we* are concerned, is stone blind to one of man's greatest desires—his longing for physical strength.

[129]

It is possible, of course, to be overly conscious of the physical. Someone has said, naïvely but truly, that women are primarily concerned with three great problems, all of which have to do with their weight: putting it on, taking it off, and rearranging it. Certainly great sums of money are spent by all of us, male and female alike, in getting well and keeping well, in adding or subtracting our avoirdupois for the sake of longer or more comfortable living. Ours is a day of patent medicines, new drugs and new cures for old diseases.

If the body is the temple of the Holy Ghost, then we surely must be interested in keeping it in good repair. We should be anxious to offer to God the finest possible dwelling place for His temple that is within our power to offer.

Does your religion work in matters of health? Do you *expect* it to work in the realm of the physical? If so, you should understand *how* it works. Christianity, you know, is the only one of the larger religions that takes the body seriously. When God wanted to explain and express Himself most fully, according to Christianity, He did so in the Incarnation—"And the Word was made flesh, and dwelt among us, and we beheld his glory, the glory as of the only begotten of the Father . . ." (A.V.). In Christ's hands we saw God moving; in His lips we heard God speaking; in the march of His feet we saw God making His way along the roads of life. He gave us the symbols of His love in terms of physical things: He gave us bread to represent His body broken for us; He gave us the cup to represent His blood poured out for our salvation. Yes, God and Christ speak to us through the medium of the physical.

And, conscious of all this, and aware that it is a "fellowship of people who care," God's church will naturally be interested in man's physical life and diseases. The church will always have a sensitive eye for the crutch, the sickbed and the wheelchair. Christ paused so often in His work and journeys to heal the sick, to give sight to the blind and to cause the lame to walk! This was not beyond the range of His interests, and it must not be beyond ours. Be it said here to the credit of the church and the churchmen of Christianity that they have always been conscious of this healing obligation. Layman Peter set the example when he stopped to heal the sick one at the gate called Beautiful, and Christian laymen since that day have been sensitive to the needs of the suffering. Hospitals are as inseparably connected with churches as apples are inseparable from a tree. The Christian hospital began in pagan Rome, where the old were thrust out to die alone, where unwanted children were abandoned. Nursing began with the patrician Christian women of the same city.

Yet, truth be told, the church has too often neglected its heritage of power to heal, and as a consequence that power has been abused and outraged at the hands of unworthy and even mercenary cults and sects which the Master would outlaw, if He could. Many of our shallow "healers" have reaped fortunes for themselves and destroyed faith in others, working in this vacuum which the careless church itself has created. But a new day is dawning. Many of the larger, major denominations are appointing commissions to study and re-study this gift of healing which was once so important a possession of the church, and of the sincere children of God.

James is quite willing that the church should become "involved" in the practice of healing. He suggests, "Is any among you sick? Let him call for the elders of the church. . . ." It is evident that healing was to be a function of the church as the official body of Christ. The word "elders," as it is used here, could not possibly be interpreted as "physicians," as some have suggested. These elders were not professional healers; they were lay *presbyters*, named to act as officials of the church. The power of effectual prayer in healing physical disease was one of their prerogatives.

There is no comfort here, of course, for those who believe in "the unorganized church." These elders represented the organized church; they were appointed in "every city," and into their hands God gave power. It was God's people who were set on special praying ground. They were not outsiders, but believers: "But as many as received him, to them he gave power to become the sons of God, even to them that believed in his name" (A.V.). It is through Christ that God becomes our Father, and it is through the Father that the healing power comes. We are told in James 5:16 that "the prayer of a *righteous* man has great power in its effects." So, before our prayers can become effective, we must be found righteous in God through Christ. This means that those who so pray have come into a position of surrender and obedience to God. These are the ones with the power, for they are the ones who stand in intimate, praying relationship with the Father.

Notice also that those who are so called and empowered are numbered in the plural; they are the elders of the church. This again suggests the power of corporate prayer. There is a principle in physics that tells us that strands of thread twisted together have greater power to lift and sustain than single strands. The twining together of our petitions in prayer guarantees a greater lifting power. The prayer prayed in the closet, in secret, is no substitute for the ones offered when two or three are gathered together, when we go to the throne of intercession hand in hand.

Here, then, we are face to face with the principle that when Christians assemble together in intercession, the prayer for healing can be highly effective.

The mention of sin in connection with healing, in

[133]

5:15, is provocative: ". . . and the prayer of faith will *save* the sick man, and the Lord will raise him up; and if he has committed sins, he will be forgiven." Some diseases are the result of sin; when this is true, it is possible that the disease will be conquered because the stimulating sin is driven out. When the disease is removed, the sin will be forgiven. In his first letter to the Corinthians, Paul says that because of the abuse or careless use of the Lord's Supper some are "weak and sickly among you." Our doctors would understand that; they have proved beyond doubt that a sense of guilt and fear inspired by committed sin can and does arrest the healing and knitting of ailing flesh and broken bones. One woman said of another, in the presence of her doctor, "She gives me a pain in the neck." To which the doctor replied, "If you go on hating her, of course you will have a pain in your neck, *because you have a Christian neck*." The doctors also tell us that a mother's milk can be poisoned in her breast—to the danger of her nursing child—when she is in a fit of anger.

Christ is co-Creator with the Father: "Without him was not anything that is made" (A.V.). If this be true, then this universe is constructed on a Godly and Christian plan, and it follows that the Christian way is the healthy way of existence in that universe. You and I cannot "break" the Commandments of God; they break us. They are not simply arbitrary commands given by deity; they are the disclosure to us of the principles on which a moral universe operates. They are *Christian* principles.

I once heard a great surgeon speak to a group of doctors. He told of how he and certain other physicians were appointed by the Federal government to draw up ten laws for public health. They debated endlessly, making little progress. Finally one of them suggested that they build their plan on the basis of the nine beatitudes of Christ's Sermon on the Mount, substituting the word "healthy" for the word "blessed." For instance—"Healthy are the pure in heart"—for sin is sand in the human machinery, and it tears a body to pieces. Or "Healthy are the peacemakers"—for disunity, hatred and jealousy within the human heart destroy the unity of the human personality. It worked, because it made sense.

The Christian thing is the healthy thing. Stomach ulcers are largely the result of worry, and the simplest cure for ulcers would seem to lie in the heeding of Christ's admonition, ". . . do not be anxious for the morrow," or in understanding that "your Father knows what you need before you ask him."

It is obvious, then, that when a sickness is the result of sin, that the sickness may be removed when the sin is removed, for a soul sick with sin means, often, a body sick with resultant physical disease. The body and the soul live so close together that they undoubtedly catch each other's diseases. Old Isaiah established this connection between soul and body when he said, "And the inhabitant shall not say, I am sick; the people that dwell therein shall be forgiven their iniquity (sin)" (A.V.). Dr. Moffat has translated other Old Testament passages thus: "A mind at ease is life and health . . . I age under outrages . . . trouble wears away my strength . . . my heart is throbbing, and the pith of life has left me." And any man knows that "a merry heart doeth good like a medicine." When you turn to the New Testament, you find innumerable instances in which a definite relationship is established between the sin of the soul and the health of the body.

But let us say once more that *all* sickness is not the result of sin. Paul had "a thorn in the flesh"—possibly trachoma, a disease of the eyes prevalent for centuries in Asia Minor. It could well have been trachoma, for the Galatians had been talking about "plucking out their eyes and giving them to him." Paul prayed thrice that God should remove this "thorn in the flesh," but each time his prayer was met with refusal. Later, Paul "gloried" in this infirmity. If this thorn were the infirmity he had in mind, then he could not have gloried in something that was the result of his sin.

Sometimes the sinner seems to prosper while the righteous suffer; we see pagans riding around in limousines, enjoying exorbitant riches and perfect health and never giving God a thought while another fine, disciplined soul, obedient to God and utterly consecrated, rides in a cripple's wheelchair. Some sinners seem to prosper; but leave them to God, whose memory is long and whose mills grind slowly. Some righteous men do seem to have suffered—but it was not because they were faithless but because they were faithful; and we must understand that they were happier suffering than a calloused sinner ever could be, living his lie. Livingstone died on his knees in an African hut, having worked himself to death for God and the African; he wouldn't have had it any other way. Frank Higgins, sky pilot to the lumberjacks of the Northwest, died of a cancer caused by the rubbing of the shoulderstraps of his knapsack, in which he carried Bibles and medicines for the men who dropped the big trees; he gave himself gladly. Doctors have died when they offered themselves as guinea pigs in experiments with fatal diseases; they wanted it that way. Christ suffered on the cross—not because He had forgotten God, but because He had remembered us. Many bodies have been consumed because too hot a flame has burned on the altar of holy consecration; their zeal burned them up. The epitaph on many a mother's tombstone could well be, "This woman died because of too much loving, washing, scrubbing and healing." "Greater love hath no man than this, that a man lay down his life for his friends" (A.V.).

We need not believe that prayer for healing rules

out medicine for healing; we have access to healing through both mediums. Why is oil used for anointing, in the Bible? Why did Christ use spittle to make clay with which to anoint the blind eyes he healed? Why was a poultice of fig leaves commanded by God to be used in the healing of an Old Testament king? Did all these instruments hold healing qualities?

There are some who think that oil, for one, certainly had healing, or at least medicinal, power. Aelius Gallus had oil applied externally to his fevered body during his last illness. Herod the Great was bathed in it when he came to death's door, according to the historian Josephus. Christ Himself relates how wine and oil were poured by the Good Samaritan into the wounds of the man he found bleeding on the road. There's a strong possibility that oil, in those days, was used as a medicinal means for the answering of prayer.

There are others who believe the use of oil was symbolic, or merely suggestive, or a means of bolstering the faith of the sufferer. Is there anything wrong with that? Cannot faith use visible means of support? The outward symbols of the bread and the wine used in the Supper bring to us a greater consciousness of our faith in the forgiving power of God through Jesus Christ. It might be possible that Biblical oil was simply a symbol of God's miraculous power, but in any event it is wise for us to remember that it is the faith of the prayer that heals, rather than the oil.

There are still others who feel that God is suggesting here the use of consecrated medicine, or medicinal means, in the work of healing. The oil was consecrated, or blessed, before it was used; it was put to the uses of God and the healing attendant upon its use became *divine* healing. One of our finest doctors says that he does not believe in any other kind of healing but divine healing. He says that he merely uses the laws which God has put into effect: "I never healed anyone; I simply made it easy for God's law to operate by getting the rubbish out of the way." When we pray for a healing we are merely getting the rubbish of sin out of the way so that the state of mind of the sick one may be opened to guidance by God's will.

More and more, the medical profession is becoming aware of the possibility that the spiritual and the physical are handmaidens together. Testimonies and evidence are piling up which more and more convince the thoughtful physicians that their greatest ally in the art of healing is the presence of God and the Great Physician. Dr. Rusche, the late president of the National Urological Society and a splendid churchman, said some time ago that "In the pursuit of scientific wizardry, we may have lost some of the heart and soul of our profession. Men of science are unbelievably intolerant and narrow when they fail to recognize that it is God's creative power, working through us, that brings success to our efforts; that the healing resources

[139]

of this universe were not invented by us. Whether or not we admit it, we are always dependent upon that Power which is greater than ourselves. Possibly the necessity of our devotion to extreme specialism has resulted in the loss of the spiritual quality and . . . has dimmed our recognition and use of one of the fundamentals of healing—namely, faith in the Divine Power. The laws of health and the moral law are parts of the same code. The Founder of Christianity tied the two together in His claim of authority: 'For whether is easier, to say, Thy sins be forgiven thee; or to say, Arise, and walk?' (A.V.). Both lie in the power of God. There is a danger of medicine yielding to an idolatry of its own techniques, to a blind unwillingness to see the wider concepts of Divinity in the world, and the danger of religion being merely a tradition inherited from the past. The laboratory and the sanctuary can become allies and creative partners. . . . Neither can satisfactorily progress alone."

What a splendid challenge this is to a partnership of the spiritual and the physical! Let us get the very best God-directed medical assistance obtainable; then in our extremity we shall also have access to that higher court of appeal which is the power of God to heal and to save.

But we must realize that we are in no position to demand healing in all cases. Conditions, or circumstances, alter cases. It is true that there is no "con-

[140]

ditioning" phrase in the statement of Jesus in Mark 11:24: ". . . What things soever ye desire, when ye pray, believe that ye receive them, and ye shall have them" (A.V.). But there is such a thing as the conditioning of parallel passages. There are other verses that throw light on this problem of intercession, and in these passages we *do* find room for a conditioning of our petitions. Whatever we ask for must be asked for according to the will of God. "Thy will be done" is the wisest accompaniment to prayer that we know.

The classic passage on prayer in the Gospel according to Luke gives evidence of the fact that God's answer will sometimes be "No." "If a son shall ask bread of any of you that is a father, will he give him a stone?" (A.V.). So often, when healing is denied after we have prayed for it, we think we have asked the Father for a loaf and been given a stone; we forget that many times what we ask for seems to be bread but is really rock: we would break our teeth upon it. ". . . Or if he asks for an egg, will give him a scorpion?" Often a scorpion looks like an egg, folded up subtly as it can be. Many times something that would seem to be an act of mercy could have the sting of death in it, if God were to let us have it. God, being a good Father, knows how to give good gifts to His children; He gives no evil gifts. Often it seems that "evil worketh good for us," and, in reverse, "seeming good would work evil for us."

[141]

It is best to put ourselves in the position of perfect trust in God, of being willing to let Him take our requests and weigh them in His all-wise hand, put some aside and give us the others according to His judgment.

Paul's prayers for healing were not always granted. He was unable to heal Epaphroditus. He left Trophimus behind at Miletus, still sick. His own "thorn in the flesh" was not removed. Study Paul! He knew the mind of Christ and the will of God, and accepted it.

Our power in prayer must *always* be conditioned by the all-wise will of God. If this were not true, then we should, by mental gymnastics and trumped-up belief, maneuver God into a corner and leave Him utterly powerless to do as He wants to do with His own universe. All death would then be arrested by our intercession; the gates of death would never open and the gates of glory never receive those who had won their crown, and God could take none to serve Him in His temple until every man should decree when he should go, and we should all find ourselves in a position to cancel out that which God has said, that ". . . it is appointed unto men once to die" (A.V.).

Many miracles of healing are beyond contradiction; it is evident that God chooses at times to heal His children as an act of mercy and as a witness to His power. We must also concede that there are other times when God asks us to bear our burdens of sickness

[142]

and suffering for His glory. May our prayer constantly be that He should deliver us from a pagan use of pain. There is a Christian use of pain; God give us the holy artistry to use it in a Christian way.

Some day, in a glorious resurrection, the perfect body shall be joined to the perfect soul. Until then, let us wear our bodies like a loose garment, never allowing them to constrict our souls. Until that great day comes, may the body and the soul be so obedient to the will of God that they should be proud of each other for all eternity. Should we be asked to wear the robes of pain for His glory, may we do so royally, with the sense that all that befalls us, when we are in His will, must touch us only within the fingers of God.

A good poet whose name I have forgotten puts it thus:

To keep a tranquil mind through days of pain,
And have a word of cheer for weary souls
Who daily cross my path. To look ahead
With courage and with faith—to bury deep
The sorrows and the failures of the past,
To see my dear ones carrying the loads
That should be mine, and not increase the weight
By useless fretting; to let hands and brain
Lie idle when the urge and zest of life
Continually challenge all their powers;
To harbor not resentment when the prize
I coveted so much has been bestowed
On someone else, because my wavering strength

[143]

Make Your Faith Work

Could not survive the rigors of the race,
And without bitterness or vain regrets
To stand and watch the world go by,
God!—if this be my task—then may I find
In doing it with gladness my reward.

My brothers, if any of you should wander away from the Truth and another should turn him back on the right path, then the latter may know that in turning a man back from his wandering course he has rescued a soul from death, and his loving action will "cover a multitude of sins."

(James 5:19, 20)
Phillips' Translation

CHAPTER IX

Are You a Soul Winner?

We come now to the matter of final values. We have seen that man is a trichotomy—a creature of body, mind and soul. We have considered the value of the mind and the body; now we consider the final value of the soul. In the last chapter we discussed the question of the power of intercession in the realm of physical healing; suppose now we think of the working of this power in the realm of spiritual salvage.

Would to God it were possible to arouse as much interest in the healing of a man's soul as we have in the healing of his body! Regrettably, it has never been thus, in human society. Just as it was easy to find four men to bring the man sick of the palsy to Jesus, to tear a hole in the roof and let him down into the healing hands of the Master, so we find it easy to bring people in multitudes to the tent of an itinerant healer today. People flock to the spectacle. They come with little urging to pray in intercession for the healing of physical man. But suppose you tell these same people that "the prayer of faith will *save* the sick" and inform

[147]

them that you are using this word "save" in a strictly spiritual sense—how many will flock together for such a purpose? To promise to heal the body brings crowds; to promise to save the soul brings a blank stare.

We spend millions on hospitals, on medical research, on efforts to cure cancer, polio and tuberculosis—and who would not thank God for that? But in comparison we spend pennies for the cure and salvage of the human soul. Some time ago a child was lost in one of our Western mountains. Two hundred Marines came in trucks from their nearby encampment to search the forest, and we all rejoiced when the child was found. But how often do we organize and deploy in the search for the *soul* of one lost child, and keep searching until the child is saved? There are twenty-seven million boys and girls in the United States without any regular religious instruction; that many young souls are imperiled and will come to spiritual death unless their desperate need is met. Yet how difficult it is to enlist Christians to comb the deserts of our populace to rescue these who are lost—to save the soul of a single child! In this day of medical miracle, we may be losing our sense of the vital.

"My brethren, if any among you wanders from the truth and some one brings him back. . . ." What pathos James pours into these words! He reminds us, sadly, that while it is possible for anyone to wander from God's truth, it is equally possible to bring him back.

". . . let him know that whoever brings back a sinner from the error of his way will save his soul from death. . . ."

There are two kinds of death. One is the insignificant death which occurs when a man's soul is separated from his body. God never overemphasizes this, for He has provided a sure way to conquer it. The other form of death is that which comes while a man yet lives on this earth—comes when a man's soul is separated from God because sin lifts its ugly head between that man and his God. Until this sin has been dissolved by an act of faith and repentance, a man exists in living death. With what enthusiasm, then, should you and I leap to restore the happy relationship which existed before this separation!

"And they that be wise shall shine as the brightness of the firmament; and they shall turn many to righteousness as the stars forever and forever" (A.V.). Why does Daniel use such enthusiastic phrases, such extreme expressions? Because the soul is thrillingly eternal, and when you touch a soul you perform an eternal work.

We must be wooed day by day to this sense of final values, in thought, in word, in action. We must restore our interest in the spiritual equation of human beings. We must see that what happens to the soul of man is of supreme importance in the mind of God.

Some years ago we asked for $128,000 to help that

[149]

army of migrant workers and families roaming over our land in trailers, in search of work that wasn't there. They needed pastoral and spiritual leadership. The money was denied—*and in the same year we spent five millions on migratory birds.* When will the day come when we will value men as highly as birds? When will the faith and souls of men mean as much as the welfare of our feathered friends?

James realized the need. In the closing verses of his Epistle he speaks strongly of the need of powerful prayer in the saving of man's soul. There were probably those who asked James, "But can we limit the grace of God in this way? Can we say that it is channeled only through our human prayers? Can we actually determine the direction of the divine love and grace by our prayers?" We can, to a great degree. Two men were discussing the power of intercessory prayer as they walked along the crown of a high hill. They came upon an aqueduct and a huge reservoir containing a large quantity of water. Said one of the men, "There you have it! In this reservoir is a lot of water—not all the water in the world, of course, but *some* of it. It has a certain viscosity and density; it is thirst-quenching and life-giving. The nature of the water is not changed as it flows through pipes to the community below us, *but those pipes determine to whom the water shall flow.* So it is with the grace of God. It cannot *all* be stored in the reservoir of our intercession, but it can be piped down by intercessory prayer to the people below our hill."

Is God moved by our intercessions? Of course He is —else why does He bid us pray? There is a sense in which the love of God and our love come together for healing and salvation. Like flint and steel, they strike a spark of spiritual revival. But they must work together. Some souls will never be saved unless and until you add your love to the love of God.

A babe is found starving in the street; you cry out, "God, feed him!" But will that child be fed unless you cooperate and lift food to his lips? A man has fallen in the street, and is unable to rise; you pray, "God, lift this man!" Will God lift him, unless you assist Him? Do we not realize that in a very real sense we are the arms and hands of God? In many instances the salvation of man waits on your aid and mine. God can, God must use our love; many of His actions are conditioned by our cooperation.

This idea of cooperation with God is expressed in a daring poetic anthropomorphism by James Stephens:

I saw God. Do you doubt it?
Do you dare doubt it?
I saw the Almighty Man. His hand
Was resting on a mountain, and
He looked upon the World and all about it;
I saw Him plainer than you see me now.
You mustn't doubt it.

[151]

He was not satisfied;
His look was all dissatisfied.
His beard swung on a wind far out of sight
Behind the world's curve, and there was light
Most fearful from His forehead, and He sighed,
"That star went always wrong, and from the start
I was dissatisfied."
He lifted up His hand—
I say He heaved a dreadful hand
Over the spinning Earth, then I said, "Stay—
You must not strike it, God; I'm in the way;
And I will never move from where I stand."
He said, "Dear child, I feared that you were dead,"
And stayed His hand.

> —James Stephens, "What Tomas Said in a Pub."
> Used by permission of The Macmillan Co.,
> Publishers.

When God's love and yours converge on a soul, things happen, since you are not only His creature but His cooperator as well. We are not only His people; we are His partners. This is the secret of "the priesthood of believers"—that tremendous power for the salvation of man which lies in corporate prayer. James had great faith in corporate prayer: "Therefore, confess your sins to one another, and pray for one another. . . ." He believed, as we should, that to discuss our spiritual burdens is to divide them, as they are shared with others. To speak of our sins and weaknesses with each other is often to find the solution for them. To pray for one another's spiritual weaknesses is often to replace them with a new strength. Would that this could become a more natural part of our human conversation!

This has become a part of the technique of Alcoholics Anonymous; A.A.'s *share* their problems. They talk over their weaknesses with people who care, and it pays off in a big way. It should be practiced more by all of us; A.A. wants no monopoly of the technique. It should be more a part of the function of friendship in the realm of the spiritual for all of us—yet how few Christians share with each other this unique privilege and power!

I have been amazed, time and again, to watch the power of collective intercession. I have seen triangles of prayer at work; I have watched two Christians join in directed prayer for the salvation of a friend, and I have seen the salvation come. Their prayer has two definite effects. First, it makes verbal and courageous the two who have prayed. Prayer brings courage to him who prays, and enables him to project his faith toward another. Here is a principle that we should never forget: if you talk to God about your friend, it will not be long before you talk to your friend about God. Try it! There is nothing that gives us more courage of utterance and the willingness to speak to another about his spiritual welfare.

The second result, of course, is the effect upon the individual for whom we pray. Each prayer from a righteous man has a tremendous lifting and pulling power to draw that soul toward the grace and goodness of God. This is the divine propulsion of prayer.

When the third person is won, the three sides of the triangle of intercession are complete. These three in turn usually turn to form a *square* of intercession, and three Christians pray for a fourth. And so on, ad infinitum. When three or four are ready and willing to carry a spiritually palsied man into the presence of Christ, there is bound to be a healing of souls. "More things are wrought by prayer than this world dreams of!"

One of the most distressing vacuums in an otherwise Christian life is often found in the lack of a prayer list —the situation in which the Christian has no one to pray for. He prays for "the salvation of the whole world"—and he may be taking in too much territory. He might better be praying for a single soul. I have discovered, while hunting in Africa, that you cannot bring down an elephant with birdshot; it is too scattered. You must concentrate the velocity of your shot at the elephant in one single, solid bullet. Too many of our prayers are birdshot prayers; they are scattered too widely. They would have greater piercing power if we were to concentrate them on one particular person or soul. This is the dynamic of definiteness.

This concern for the soul of individual man is not something optional in our living. The task of conversion is not to make converts; it is to make evangelists. For instance—the moment the woman at the well in Samaria discovered Jesus Christ to be the Messiah, she immediately went and told the whole village about it. It is not something we can keep to ourselves. We must spread the Good News of God in Christ; He is too good to contain. If He indwells in us, He must of necessity overflow us. If He does not overflow us, He does not indwell in us! The saved soul immediately wants to save; the convert rushes to convert. No one can keep Christ unless he passes Him on. These are the inevitables of the Christian life. This is the recruiting force of our faith.

". . . let him know that whoever brings back a sinner from the error of his way will save his soul from death and cover a multitude of sins." Does this mean that the intercessor will save his own soul as he strives to save the soul of another? Not necessarily! You and I do not save our own souls simply because we help in saving another soul: *we must confess our own sins, and look to our own salvation.* It is like the cancer specialist of whom I read some time ago; he fought the dread disease in others, and he cured many of his patients when he treated the sickness in its early stages —and then he died of cancer himself! We can all die of the sins we fight in others, if we are not as mindful of sin in ourselves as we are of sin in them.

Religion is a desperately personal thing. "If any man

will come after me, let him deny *himself,* and take up *his* cross, and follow me" (A.V.). Our salvation is dependent upon personal experience, and no amount of love for another man's soul can substitute for the love and concern we have for our own. The two must go together. Too many men have said, "Take my wife and let her be consecrated, Lord, to Thee"—thinking that the home can be stabilized spiritually so long as the men do the paying and the women do the praying! It is tragic nonsense; our sins are outwitted and our souls are saved only when we confess them for ourselves and personally seek the forgiveness of God.

There is, however, a sense in which we do save ourselves as we save others. Certainly we "cover a multitude of sins" when we seek out the lost among our fellows; we may rid ourselves, at least in part, of the sins of unconcern and indifference and coldness and lovelessness when we do that. We often need the poor more than they need us, for when we save them from the threat of poverty and starvation we save ourselves from the sin of selfishness. It is doubtful if a man can gain salvation for himself if he be totally uninterested in the salvation of others.

By having a great concern for others we save our souls from the death of lovelessness. I wonder if the cross of Christ ever becomes really operative in our lives until it destroys our silence? The message of the cross is something that tolerates no silence; *it must be passed on.* Clamping its mailed fist over the mouth of

Paul, Rome said to him, "You must not speak. Be quiet!" And Paul replied, "Woe is me if I preach not the gospel!" He preached it; he was murdered for preaching it, but he lived on after his physical death to make Rome tremble with his preaching. Calvary must murder our silence as we stand upon it and consider human need.

Elizabeth Cheney puts it poignantly:

Whenever there is a silence around me
By day or by night—
I am startled by a cry.
It came down from the cross—
The first time I heard it.
I went out and searched—
And found a man in the throes of crucifixion,
And I said, "I will take you down,"
And I tried to take the nails out of his feet.
But he said, "Let them be
For I cannot be taken down
Until every man, every woman, and every child
Come together to take me down."
And I said, "But I cannot hear you cry.
What can I do?"
And he said, "Go about the world—
Tell everyone you meet—
There is a man on the cross."
　　　　　　　—Elizabeth Cheney,
　　　　　　　"There is a Man on the Cross."

Until Calvary has murdered our silence, I wonder if we have heard His voice at all.

God makes us captives of this great concern. When our religion works, we work for the salvation of others. When we are saved, we must save others. It was John Calvin who said, "We must take heed lest our souls perish through our sloth, whose salvation God puts, in a manner, in our hands. Not that we can bestow salvation on them, but that God, by our ministry, delivers and saves those who seem otherwise to be nigh destruction."

A dog was run over by a car. A doctor hurriedly bound up its broken leg and took the dog into his own home. After weeks of care he was surprised to discover that the dog had just walked off and left him. He had some harsh words to say about the ungrateful dog. Two days later he heard a scratching at his front door; on the front porch he found the dog he had healed— in company with another animal that had been hurt. Ours should surely be as great a love as this—a love that passes on the blessed information that there is One who can bind up our wounds and make us whole again.

Of all the questions that may be asked of us when we reach heaven, I think the most terrible must be this: "Did you come alone? If so, how could you?" God grant that when we come to the gates of the Eternal City we shall have brought someone with us!

What regret would then be mine
When I meet my Lord Divine,

[158]

If I've wasted all the talents He doth lend!
If no soul to me can say,
"I am glad you passed my way,
For 'twas you who told me of the sinners' Friend."

". . . whoever brings back a sinner from the error of his way will save his soul from death. . . ." What a glorious salvage! What a privilege this is! It is the crux, the crown, the great end, the final great meaning of Christ and the Christian life.